MODERN JEWISH BAKER

MODERN JEWISH BAKER

CHALLAH, BABKA, BAGELS & MORE

Shannon Sarna

The Countryman Press

A division of W. W. Norton & Company

Independent Publishers Since 1923

For my mom, and for Dana

CONTENTS

INTRODUCTION 6

TECHNIQUES, TOOLS, TOPPINGS, AND FILLINGS 9

CHALLAH 29

BABKA 89

BAGELS 141

RUGELACH 163

HAMANTASCHEN 187

PITA BREAD 213

MATZAH 233

ACKNOWLEDGMENTS 249

INDEX 251

ABOUT THE AUTHOR 263

INTRODUCTION

How does a half-Italian, half-Jewish girl from upstate New York become a challah expert and baker, and cookbook writer? I have reflected upon the unusual path my life has taken many times while putting these recipes together.

I have worked in restaurants and taken tons of recreational classes in knife skills and bread baking and cake decorating, but I am far from a chef. In fact, I started blogging about food and developing my own recipes primarily as a hobby almost 10 years ago, when I was working as a communications manager for renowned Jewish philanthropist Edgar M. Bronfman Sr., of blessed memory. But even before I began blogging and writing about food, my story truly started with baking challah.

When I was 16 years old my mother passed away from non-Hodgkin's lymphoma, and suddenly I was de facto in charge of a 13-year-old (my brother Jon) and a 6-year-old (my sister Riana). To say I didn't know what I was doing would be an understatement, but I decided I was going to start baking challah on Thursday nights with my siblings. Even though my mother wasn't Jewish (she was a nice Italian Catholic girl from Brooklyn) and I had never ever seen her make challah, she loved baking and so being in the kitchen connected me to her. One day I opened up her copy of *Beard on Bread* and I started making challah.

For the first few years, I made a lot of bad challah. Challah that was burnt on the bottom. Challah that was raw on the inside. But I just kept making it, picking up tricks and techniques along the way, until it wasn't bad, until it was pretty good. Finally, I perfected my recipe and people started asking if they could buy their Shabbat loaves from me. I was proud of the beautiful traditional challahs I was now able to produce. But they didn't remain traditional for too long.

I found myself thinking about all the wild variations I could make. It started simple enough with ingredients like rosemary and garlic, dried cherries and olive tapenade. But I was now on a challah high and I wanted to try more combinations: challah stuffed with pastrami and Russian dressing; topped with frosting and sprinkles; and even baked around an entire wheel of Brie. My challah baking expanded to cookies, which led me to babka and rugelach and other types of bread, and then chicken soup and brisket, and well, you get the picture.

As my skills became more refined, and as I took on my current role as editor of the food blog *The Nosher,* I connected with other bakers and cooks from all over the world whose "mixed" stories resonated with my own. Their expertise further encouraged me to go beyond challah. I met Jennifer Stempel, a fellow baker and blogger, whose "Jewban"

(Jewish + Cuban) creations of Latin-inspired brisket, challah, and matzah ball soup further inspired me to use my own Italian heritage in more of my creations.

I learned to make hamantaschen from Rachel Korycan and her mom Susan, a convert to Judaism, whose hamantaschen recipe was the best I ever tasted. Over the years I adapted her recipe, expanding and creating classic and crazy flavors for Purim each year.

I met Samantha Ferraro, a blogger from the West Coast, who taught me to make rugelach, a task with which I had previously struggled. Samantha, whose mother was Sephardi and father was Ashkenazi, was raised in Hawaii and later married a man of Italian descent. She mixes the diverse influences from her life into some of the most beautiful, colorful, and delicious creations. These are just a few of the creative women I have connected with over the years who are reclaiming and reinventing traditional foods with modern and multi-ethnic interpretations.

Bagels, pita, and matzah have been new additions to my baking repertoire. I must admit that I initially considered these baking tasks daunting, but once I started making my own pita, bagel, and matzah creations, I could never return to store-bought. Making these breads has become as addictive as my desire to create new flavors of challah.

A few years ago I was at a Jewish food event when a colleague came up to me and asked, "What is it about challah for you? Why do you make so many different kinds?" It was an interesting question, and one that I hadn't given much thought to before that moment. She went on to explain that she grew up eating the same traditional challah that her mom made every week, and now she happily makes the same plain challah every week for her own family. Of course there are many Jewish families who savor the taste of and the process of baking challah for the very fact that it is, in its original form, traditional and familiar. For them, challah is sweet in its simplicity. For me, however, maybe because my own history is not typical, I see challah as a way to merge old and new, and create something that is comforting but also unexpected.

My intention for this cookbook echoes my sentiment about challah—I want it to both serve as a sort of baking map for you to master different types of dough and also be an invitation to be creative and diverse. These recipes are expressions of my not-so-uniquely mixed up American Jewishness; and they are inspired by my own Italian-Jewish upbringing, my many travels to Israel, and the many other "mixed" Jews I have known who mash up their different cultural identities into delicious, meaningful, and unique food.

TECHNIQUES, TOOLS, TOPPINGS, AND FILLINGS

We are in a wonderful moment in time when considering baked goods. No longer are we shackled to just one idea of what a bagel/challah/rugelach/babka must look and taste like. While I would like to consider myself a baking trailblazer, the trend of elevating and reinterpreting challah, rugelach, babka, and hamantaschen has been happening all over the country for some time: savory rugelach in Los Angeles, pulled brisket stuffed babka in Brooklyn, and red velvet challah in Boston, just to name a few. And that's not even mentioning the secular carb counterparts of cupcakes, croissants, doughnuts, and their many iterations.

The recipes in this book should serve as gentle guiding suggestions, but by no means are they precisely prescriptive and written in stone. There is no limit to the flavor pairings and combinations. Enjoy the toppings, fillings, and dough infusions I suggest in each chapter, but then have fun and play around with the combinations that most appeal to you. Master each dough, mix it up, and make it your own.

Pay attention to the list of tools at the beginning of each chapter and the type of flour, because these things do matter. In baking, one cannot skip steps; precision matters, and the right tools and ingredients can make the difference between something average and something extraordinary.

Keep in mind that the time of year can greatly impact dough, especially yeasted doughs like challah, babka, bagels, and pita. During the summer when it is more humid, recipes may require slightly more flour to achieve the same result you'd get in a different season. In the winter, a recipe might need slightly less flour than normal. If your kitchen (like mine) is a bit cold, getting dough to rise easily might be a challenge. A warm oven provides the solution. Try a trick that several of my baking friends use: Warm the oven to 200°F, turn it off, and then place dough (like challah, babka, or pita dough) in the oven so that it will rise more quickly.

Exact baking time for all these recipes will vary from oven to oven. If you're not sure about the exactness of your oven, buy an oven thermometer and check the accuracy. The behavior of your oven will make a difference in the time and temperature you choose for your baking projects.

PIZZA STONE

SILPAT

made in France   150   emarle

SILPAT

MEASURING CUP

MEASURING CUP

BRUSH

TOWEL

WHISK

ROLLING PIN

SPATULA

WOODEN SPOON

SCALE

SPATULA

PASTA ROLLER

PIZZA CUTTER

DOUGH CUTTER

CUTTING BOARD

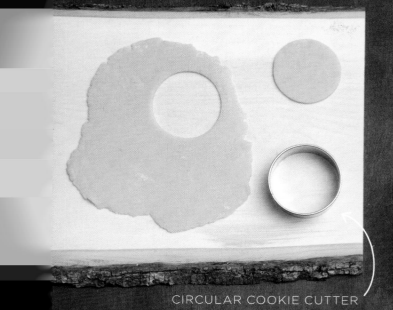

MEASURING SPOON

CIRCULAR COOKIE CUTTER

BAKING PAN

FORK

BOWL

ROLLING PIN

WIRE COOLING RACK

WIRE STRAINER

TONGS

BAKING SHEET

TOPPINGS

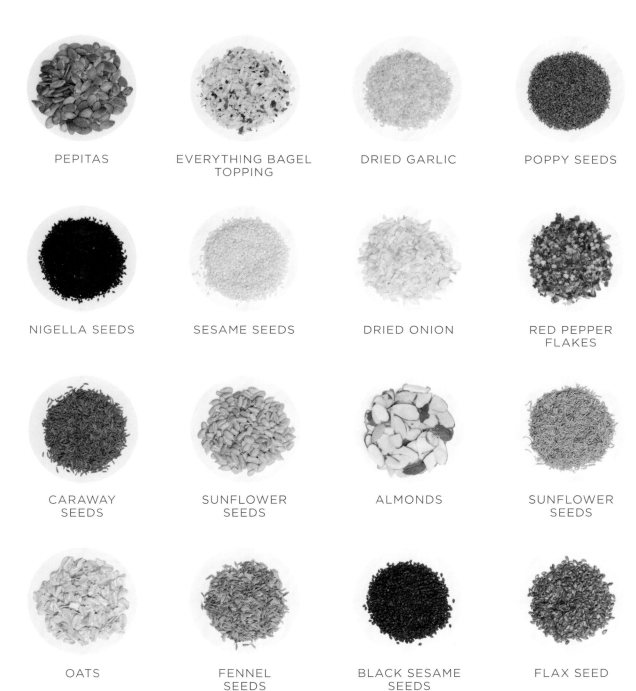

PEPITAS

EVERYTHING BAGEL
TOPPING

DRIED GARLIC

POPPY SEEDS

NIGELLA SEEDS

SESAME SEEDS

DRIED ONION

RED PEPPER
FLAKES

CARAWAY
SEEDS

SUNFLOWER
SEEDS

ALMONDS

SUNFLOWER
SEEDS

OATS

FENNEL
SEEDS

BLACK SESAME
SEEDS

FLAX SEED

TOPPINGS AND FILLINGS

There is no shortage of fillings and toppings to adorn your baked goods, but I decided to include some of my very favorite recipes and garnishes.

EVERYTHING BAGEL TOPPING

Everything bagel topping is pretty trendy these days, with bakers and bloggers putting it on everything from dough-nuts to pizza crust to croissants. I love using this topping for loaves of challah, individual challah rolls, challah dogs, and even savory rugelach. This amount makes enough for two loaves of challah, but you can easily double or triple it to have a large batch on hand.

Yields ⅔ cup

INGREDIENTS

2 tablespoons sesame seeds

2 tablespoons black sesame seeds

2 tablespoons poppy seeds

2 tablespoons dried garlic pieces

2 tablespoons dried onion pieces

1 tablespoon coarse sea salt

1 heaping teaspoon red pepper flakes (optional)

INSTRUCTIONS

Add all ingredients to a small bowl and combine. Store in an air-tight container for up to 2 to 3 months.

SPICED SUGAR

Cinnamon sugar is an easy enough ingredient to throw together. But by adding some extra spices and salt, you can bring a delicious sweet and salty complexity to sweet challah, rugelach, and hamantaschen.

Yields about ½ cup

INGREDIENTS

½ cup sugar

1½ tablespoons cinnamon

½ teaspoon nutmeg

¼ teaspoon ground cloves

¼ teaspoon sea salt

INSTRUCTIONS

Add all ingredients to a small bowl and combine. Store in an airtight container for up to 2 to 3 months.

CRUMB TOPPING

This crumb topping is inspired by Ina Garten's classic blueberry coffee cake. My family became so enthralled with the crumb topping, I started adding it on top of babka and other sweets. You could also try adding this to the top of a sweet challah or even rugelach for something truly decadent.

Yields about 2½ cups

INGREDIENTS

¼ cup sugar

⅓ cup packed brown sugar

½ cup (1 stick) unsalted butter, melted

1⅓ cups unbleached all-purpose flour

¼ teaspoon fine sea salt

INSTRUCTIONS

Place all ingredients in a bowl. Using a wooden spoon, mix until crumbs form. Sprinkle on top of sweet babka or challah before baking.

KALE BASIL WALNUT PESTO

Pesto is an easy enough condiment to buy at the supermarket. But when summer comes and greens are in abundance, I love turning kale, spinach, and other greens into homemade pesto. You can replace the kale with 3 cups fresh spinach or use pine nuts instead of walnuts, if you want something more traditional. If you have leftover pesto, it makes a great seasoning for chicken or sauce for pasta.

Yields about 2 cups

INGREDIENTS

¼ cup chopped walnuts

2 cups fresh kale, rib and stems removed

1 cup fresh basil leaves

3 garlic cloves

⅓ cup good quality olive oil

INSTRUCTIONS

In a sauté pan on low-medium heat, slowly toast walnuts until just fragrant, about 3 minutes. Make sure they do not burn. When you can smell the nuts, they are done.

Bring a large pot of water to boil. Prepare a large bowl filled with cold water and ice cubes.

Plunge kale into boiling water and let it sit for 1 minute. Remove and place immediately into the ice water. After 5 minutes, remove the kale and carefully remove excess water.

In a food processor fitted with a blade, add kale, basil, walnuts, garlic, and a few tablespoons of the olive oil. Begin to pulse. Slowly add the remaining olive oil until smooth. You might want to add a touch more olive oil depending on your preference.

MIXED OLIVE TAPENADE

Olive tapenade is a classic Mediterranean condiment—perfect on crostini, an ideal accompaniment on a cheese platter, and, of course, delicious when stuffed inside savory babka or bite-sized hamanaschen. You can also try making tapenade with just Kalamata olives. Since both olives and anchovy filets are salty, I recommend tasting before adding too much additional salt.

Yields about 2 cups

INGREDIENTS

½ pound mixed pitted olives

3 anchovy fillets, rinsed (can substitute 2 teaspoons anchovy paste)

2 garlic cloves

¼ cup good quality olive oil

Salt and pepper to taste

INSTRUCTIONS

Place all ingredients in a food processor fitted with a blade attachment. Pulse until smooth. Store in airtight container in the refrigerator for up to one month.

SAVORY ONION JAM

Onion jam may sound a bit like an oxymoron, but it is an addictive condiment that you will be slathering on everything from grilled cheese sandwiches to savory rugelach. Make sure to cook the onions on low heat, otherwise they may burn and get a bitter taste. You can experiment by adding a few cloves of roasted garlic or some fresh herbs to the food processor.

Yields about 2 cups

INGREDIENTS

3 tablespoons olive oil

3 large onions, sliced (you can use yellow or red onions)

2 teaspoons sugar

½ teaspoon salt

¼ teaspoon pepper

1 tablespoon balsamic vinegar

INSTRUCTIONS

Heat olive oil in a large pan over medium-low heat. Add onions and cook over low heat for about 15 minutes. Add sugar, salt, and pepper and keep stirring on low heat for another 15 to 20 minutes.

Add balsamic vinegar and cook for 2 to 3 more minutes.

After onions have cooled, place in a food processor fitted with a blade attachment. Pulse until smooth. Store in airtight container in fridge until ready to use. Jam will last in refrigerator for up to 2 weeks.

CINNAMON SUGAR FILLING

This cinnamon sugar filling may not seem like much, but stuffed inside challah dough, or shmeared inside rugelach, and it quickly becomes a decadent baked treat. In the fall replace the cinnamon with pumpkin pie spice to usher in the smell and taste of autumn.

Yields about 2 cups

INGREDIENTS

¾ cup (1½ sticks) unsalted butter, melted

1½ cups sugar

2 tablespoons cinnamon

Pinch salt

INSTRUCTIONS

Combine all ingredients in a bowl. Use to spread inside babka, challah, or rugelach.

CHOCOLATE FILLING

Rich chocolate swirled babka is the breakfast, brunch, or teatime treat we all crave, and this chocolate filling is perfect for a sweet and simple chocolate babka. But it's also perfect stuffed inside challah, rugelach, and hamantaschen. Always use good-quality chocolate and cocoa powder (at least 60% cocoa) for the best result.

Yields about 2 cups

INGREDIENTS

6 ounces dark chocolate, cut into pieces (or good quality dark chocolate chips, such as Ghirardelli)

¾ cup (1½ sticks) unsalted butter, at room temperature

½ cup sugar

⅓ cup cocoa powder (I recommend Hershey's Special Dark Cocoa powder)

¼ teaspoon cinnamon

Pinch fine sea salt

INSTRUCTIONS

In a microwave-safe bowl, heat chocolate in 30-second intervals until completely melted, stirring vigorously in between with a small spatula. Allow to cool for 2 minutes.

Beat butter and sugar until smooth. Add cocoa powder, melted dark chocolate, cinnamon, and salt. Use to spread inside babka, challah, or rugelach.

CHALLAH

Challah is one of the most iconic and uniquely Jewish foods. The time Jews spent in Europe, however, may have most heavily influenced its current iteration. Regardless, the concept of a braided bread on the Sabbath is one that is truly Jewish and sacred. Some varieties of challah are more akin to cake, using eggs, oil, and sugar; whereas other varieties rely exclusively on water, yeast, oil, and flour. Jews picked up dishes and ingredients and inspiration from the many places where our people have lived over many thousands of years, and challah is one of our foods that reflects the diversity of our people and those experiences.

The secret about challah I want to share with you is that, while for some people it is an intimidating baking task, it is one of the most forgiving breads you can bake. It doesn't require fermentation, and even the worst homemade challah is still delicious and intoxicating. Challah is sort of like tofu—it will take on the flavor of whatever you put in it. It can be fancy, it can be simple, and from where I sit, it is very open to being influenced by the flavors and textures that you find most pleasing.

My other secret about challah is that it has less to do with the actual recipe itself, and more about tools and technique. If you like your challah doughier, bake it at 350°F. If you like it with a good crust and fluffier, bake it at 375°F.

Note: To keep your yeast fresh, make sure to store it in the fridge.

HOW THE DOUGH SHOULD FEEL

Challah dough should feel easy to work with in your hands, but not completely loose. It should maintain shape well, but if it's too hard to roll out or shape, it may be too dense when baked. When adding flour to challah dough, sometimes less is more. If you poke the challah dough, you should see a small indent and then it should bounce back slightly.

RISING

To achieve fluffy challah, you must allow the dough to rise two times. The first rise should be 2 to 3 hours at room temperature, or you can place in a greased bowl with plastic wrap over the top and allow it to rise overnight in the fridge. After braiding (or shaping) the challah, it should rise again for another 30 to 45 minutes, but no longer. There are a few ways to get your challah to rise a bit faster, if you need to save time. You can heat your oven to 200°F, turn it off, and then pop your dough (covered with a damp towel) in the oven for 1½ hours. You can also run a kitchen towel under hot water, squeeze out the excess water, and drape over the top of the bowl. If your kitchen tends to be cold (like mine), try turning the oven on to warm up the kitchen. On the other hand, if it's hot and humid outside, you can stick your challah right outside, covered with a damp towel, for a faster rise.

STORAGE

Allow challah to cool completely on a drying rack before storing. If not serving right away, place in a sealable plastic bag. It should be noted that challah is always best when eaten within 1 to 2 days of baking. If freezing, wrap in foil then place in a freezer bag as soon as the challah cools. If you opt to freeze challah, before serving allow it to defrost and then pop in a warm oven (200°F) for 10 to 15 minutes.

FLOUR

I recommend using a high-gluten flour for challah, more specifically, King Arthur bread flour. You can use an all-purpose flour, and I did for many years before switching to bread flour, but the bread flour will yield a higher gluten level and better crumb.

ESSENTIAL TOOLS

If you want to make challah that looks as delicious as it tastes, the number one tool I recommend is a **digital scale**. After your dough rises, use your scale to measure each strand precisely. The more exact all the strands, the more uniform the challah will be and therefore more beautiful.

Invest in a good **silicone baking mat** such as the Silpat brand. They last a long time and they ensure an easy cleanup with no burnt or sticking bottoms of your bread.

Some people like silicone brushes for egg wash, but I despise them. Go old school and buy a **wooden pastry brush** for more even brushing.

BASIC CHALLAH BRAID

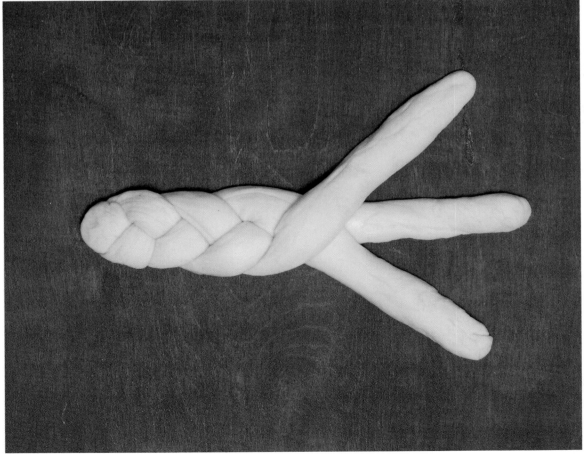

3-STRAND ROUND CHALLAH

 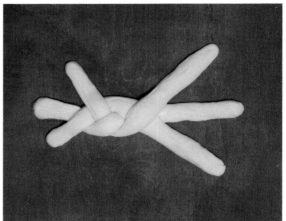

6-STRAND CHALLAH BRAID

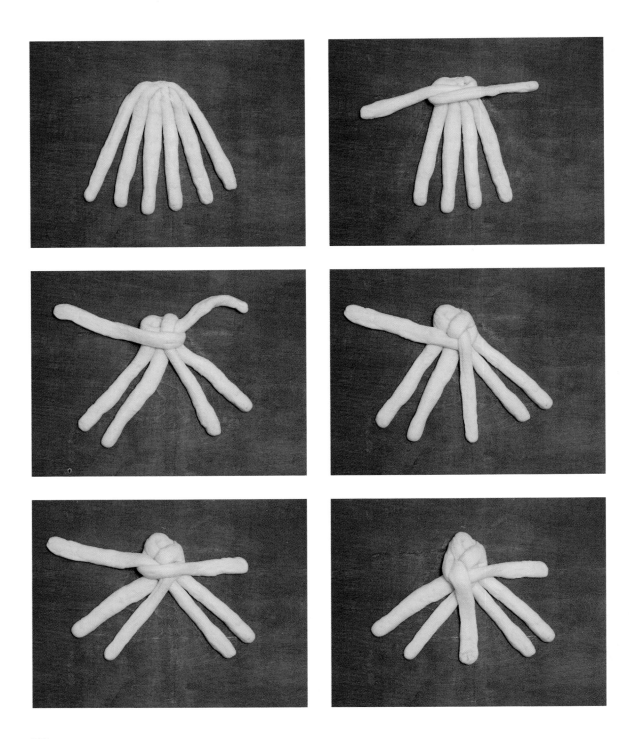

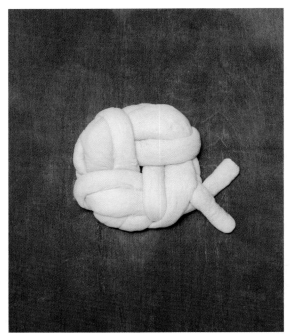

CHALLAH KNOTS

STUFFED 3-STRAND CHALLAH

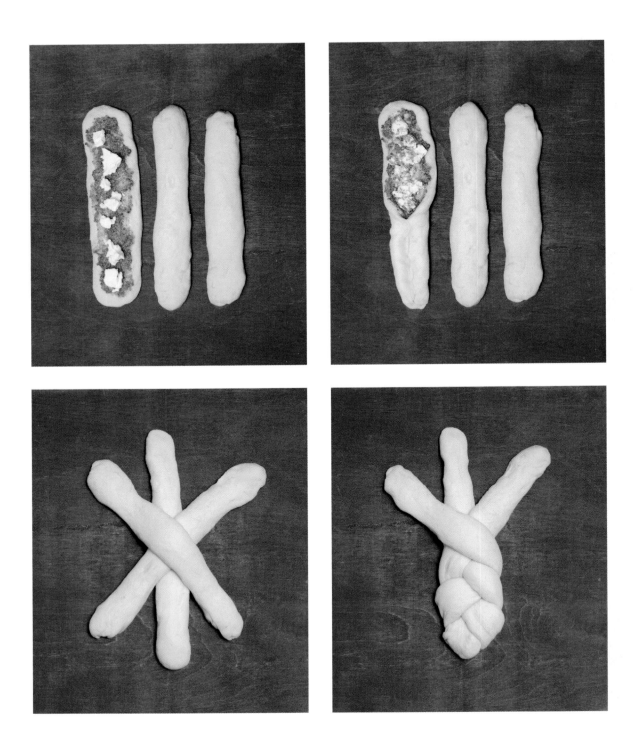

STUFFED TURBAN CHALLAH

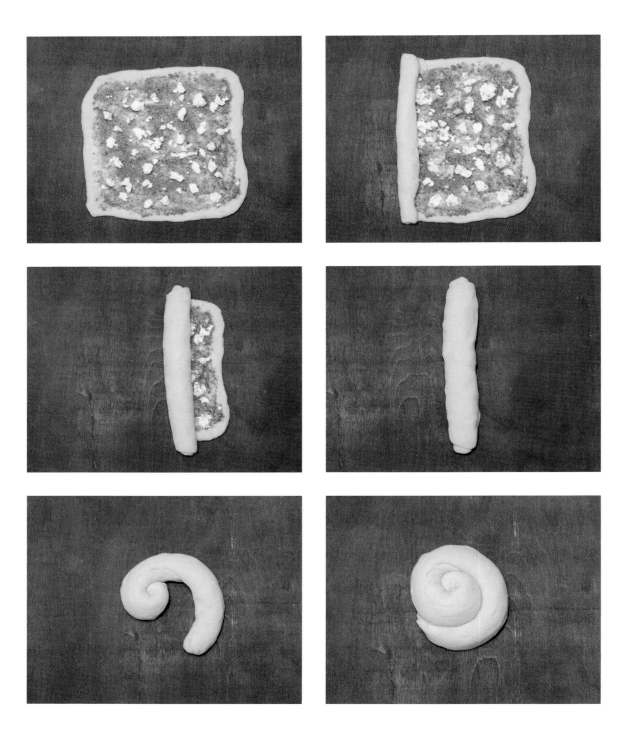

BASIC CHALLAH

Even without any additional spices, stuffing, or adornments, simple, basic challah is one of the most comforting and gratifying foods. My basic recipe is a little sweet, with a beautiful shiny exterior and chewy interior. If you prefer challah that is less sweet, you can reduce the amount of sugar in this recipe to $1/3$ cup. If you prefer to use olive oil over vegetable oil, then do so using the exact same measurements. The result will be just as delicious.

Yields 2 medium loaves

INGREDIENTS

FOR THE DOUGH:

1½ tablespoons dry active yeast

½ cup + 2 tablespoons + ½ teaspoon sugar

1¼ cups lukewarm water

4½–5 cups unbleached bread flour (preferably King Arthur)

½ tablespoon fine sea salt

¼ cup vegetable oil

2 large eggs

FOR THE TOPPING:

2 egg yolks (or 1 whole egg)

1 teaspoon water

¼ teaspoon coarse sea salt (optional)

2–3 tablespoons sesame seeds (optional)

2–3 tablespoons poppy seeds (optional)

INSTRUCTIONS

For the dough: In a small bowl, place the yeast, ½ teaspoon sugar, and lukewarm water. Stir gently to mix. Allow to sit 5 to 10 minutes, until it becomes foamy on top.

In a large bowl or stand mixer fitted with the whisk attachment, mix together 1½ cups of the flour, salt, and ½ cup plus 2 table-spoons sugar. Add the water-yeast mixture and oil to flour. Mix thoroughly.

Add another 1 cup of the flour and eggs and mix until smooth. Switch to the dough hook attachment if you are using a stand mixer.

Add another 1½ to 2 cups of the flour and mix thoroughly. Then remove dough from the bowl and place on a floured surface. Knead the remaining ½ cup flour into dough, continuing to knead for about 5 minutes.

Place dough in a greased bowl and cover with a damp towel. Allow to rise at least 3 hours.

Divide the dough in two and braid the challahs into desired shape. See pages 32–45 for braiding.

Place braided challah on a baking sheet lined with parchment paper or silicone baking mat. Allow the challah to rise another 45 to 60 minutes, or until you can see the size has grown and the challah seems light. This step is very important to ensure a light and fluffy challah. Preheat oven to 375°F while the dough rises.

For the topping: In a small bowl beat 2 egg yolks with 1 tea-spoon water. Brush the egg wash liberally over challah. Sprinkle with coarse sea salt, sesame seeds, or poppy seeds if desired.

Bake 24 to 26 minutes, or until the color is golden.

WHOLE-GRAIN CHALLAH

Instead of using 100 percent whole-wheat bread flour in this recipe, I use a mix of flours: unbleached white bread flour, whole-wheat bread flour, and oat bran (which adds sweetness and some health benefits too). I encourage you to play around with your flour mix to include rye flour, spelt flour, buckwheat flour, or others depending on your preferences.

Yields 2 medium loaves

INGREDIENTS

FOR THE DOUGH:

1½ tablespoons dry active yeast

1 teaspoon sugar, divided

1¼ cups lukewarm water

2½ cups unbleached bread flour (preferably King Arthur)

1½ cups whole-wheat bread flour (can also use regular whole-wheat flour)

½ cup oat bran

1½ teaspoons salt

½ cup sugar

¼ cup vegetable oil

2 large eggs

INSTRUCTIONS

For the dough: In a small bowl, place the yeast, ½ teaspoon sugar, and lukewarm water. Stir gently to mix. Allow to sit 5 to 10 minutes, until it becomes foamy on top.

In a large bowl or stand mixer fitted with the whisk attachment, mix together 1 cup of the unbleached bread flour with ½ cup of the whole-wheat flour, the oat bran, salt, and sugar. Add the water-yeast mixture and oil to flour. Mix thoroughly.

Add another ½ cup of the bread flour, ½ cup of the whole-wheat flour, and 2 eggs and mix until smooth. Switch to the dough hook attachment if you are using a stand mixer.

Add the remaining flour and mix until dough comes together. It should feel slightly dense and just a tad sticky.

Remove from bowl and place on a lightly floured surface. Hand knead for 30 seconds, just until dough is smooth and no longer sticky.

Place in a large greased bowl. Drape a warm, wet dish towel over the top and allow to rise 3 hours.

Divide the dough in two and braid the challahs into desired shape. See pages 32–45 for braiding.

Place braided challah on a baking sheet lined with parchment paper or silicone baking mat. Allow the challah to rise another 45 to 60 minutes, or until you can see the size has grown and the challah seems light. This step is very important to ensure a light and fluffy challah. Preheat oven to 375°F while the dough rises.

Note: To ensure the freshness of your whole-wheat flour, make sure to store it in the freezer. Allow the whole-wheat flour to sit out at room temperature 20 to 30 minutes before using to make bread. Cold flour can slow down the rising process.

FOR THE TOPPING:

1 egg yolk (or 1 whole egg)

1 teaspoon water

¼ cup whole oats (optional)

2 tablespoons whole flaxseed (optional)

¼ teaspoon coarse sea salt (optional)

¼ cup sunflower seeds (optional)

¼ cup sliced almonds (optional)

For the topping: In a small bowl beat egg yolk with 1 teaspoon water.

Brush the egg wash liberally over challah. Sprinkle with whole oats, whole flaxseed, or other desired toppings such as coarse sea salt, sunflower seeds, or almonds.

Bake 24 to 26 minutes, or until the color is golden.

EVERYTHING BAGEL CHALLAH

Everything bagels are pretty classic, especially if you grew up in the Northeast area of the United States. And yet, the everything bagel topping has been quite trendy in the past few years: writers and chefs have created dozens of everything-flavored dishes from hummus and chicken dishes to doughnuts and even croissants. One of my favorite bakeries, Montclair Bread Company, located in Montclair, New Jersey, features a cream cheese–filled spicy everything croissant that I adore. They add a touch of red pepper flakes to the everything bagel topping, which I immediately included in my own version (see the Everything Bagel Topping on page 14). If you don't like extra spice, the red pepper flakes are completely optional.

Yields 2 medium loaves

INGREDIENTS

FOR THE DOUGH:

1½ tablespoons dry active yeast

½ cup + 2 tablespoons + ½ teaspoon sugar

1¼ cups lukewarm water

4½–5 cups unbleached bread flour (preferably King Arthur)

1½ teaspoons table salt

¼ cup vegetable oil

1 tablespoon jarred minced garlic in oil

2 teaspoons onion powder

2 large eggs

FOR THE TOPPING:

2 egg yolks (or 1 whole egg)

1 teaspoon water

⅓–½ cup Everything Bagel Topping (page 14)

INSTRUCTIONS

For the dough: In a small bowl, place the yeast, ½ teaspoon sugar, and lukewarm water. Stir gently to mix. Allow to sit 5 to 10 minutes, until it becomes foamy on top.

In a large bowl or stand mixer fitted with the whisk attachment, mix together 1½ cups of the flour, salt, and ½ cup plus 2 tablespoons sugar. Add the water-yeast mixture, oil, minced garlic, and onion powder to flour. Mix thoroughly.

Add another 1 cup of the flour and 2 eggs and mix until smooth. Switch to the dough hook attachment if you are using a stand mixer.

Add another 1½ to 2 cups of the flour and mix thoroughly. Remove from bowl and place on a floured surface. Knead the remaining ½ cup flour into dough, continuing to knead for about 5 minutes.

Place dough in a greased bowl and cover with a damp towel. Allow to rise at least 3 hours.

Divide the dough in two and braid the challahs into desired shape. See pages 32–45 for braiding.

Place braided challah on a baking sheet lined with parchment paper or silicone baking mat. Allow the challah to rise another 45 to 60 minutes, or until you can see the size has grown and the challah seems light. This step is very important to ensure a light and fluffy challah. Preheat oven to 375°F while the dough rises.

For the topping: In a small bowl beat 2 egg yolks with 1 teaspoon water. Brush the egg wash liberally over challah. Sprinkle with Everything Bagel Topping.

Bake 24 to 26 minutes, or until the color is golden.

ROSEMARY GARLIC CHALLAH

When I first started experimenting with challah varieties, rosemary and garlic was one of the first flavor combinations I tried, a nod to my dual Italian-Jewish heritage. The rosemary and coarse sea salt on top is not only delicious, but the combination produces a strikingly beautiful, but simple, challah. You don't have to use fresh rosemary—it is just as beautiful if you use dried rosemary.

Yields 2 medium loaves

INGREDIENTS

FOR THE DOUGH:

1½ tablespoons dry active yeast

½ cup + 2 tablespoons + ½ teaspoon sugar

1¼ cups lukewarm water

4½–5 cups unbleached bread flour (preferably King Arthur)

1½ teaspoons table salt

¼ cup vegetable oil

2 tablespoons dried rosemary

1 tablespoon jarred minced garlic in oil

2 large eggs

INSTRUCTIONS

For the dough: In a small bowl, place the yeast, ½ teaspoon sugar, and lukewarm water. Stir gently to mix. Allow to sit 5 to 10 minutes, until it becomes foamy on top.

In a large bowl or stand mixer fitted with the whisk attachment, mix together 1½ cups of the flour, salt, and ½ cup plus 2 tablespoons sugar. Add the water-yeast mixture, oil, dried rosemary, and minced garlic to flour. Mix thoroughly.

Add another 1 cup of the flour and 2 eggs and mix until smooth. Switch to the dough hook attachment if you are using a stand mixer.

Add another 1½ to 2 cups of flour, mix thoroughly, then remove from the bowl and place on a floured surface. Knead the remaining ½ cup flour into dough, continuing to knead for about 5 minutes.

Place dough in a greased bowl and cover with a damp towel. Allow to rise at least 3 hours.

Divide the dough in two and braid the challahs into desired shape. See pages 32–45 for braiding.

Place braided challah on a baking sheet lined with parchment paper or silicone baking mat. Allow the challah to rise another 45 to 60 minutes, or until you can see the size has grown and the challah seems light. This step is very important to ensure a light and fluffy challah. Preheat oven to 375°F while the dough rises.

FOR THE TOPPING:

2 egg yolks (or 1 whole egg)

1 teaspoon water

1 teaspoon dried rosemary or 3–4 fresh rosemary sprigs

½ teaspoon minced, dried garlic flakes

¼ teaspoon coarse sea salt

For the topping: In a small bowl beat 2 egg yolks with 1 teaspoon water. Brush the egg wash liberally over the challah. Sprinkle with the additional dried rosemary, minced garlic flakes, and coarse sea salt. If using whole fresh rosemary sprigs, run them under cold water briefly and pat dry gently. For a particularly artful presentation, place the whole rosemary sprigs on top of the glazed challah.

Bake 24 to 26 minutes, or until the color is golden.

ZA'ATAR AND GARLIC CHALLAH

Za'atar is a popular Middle Eastern spice with a pretty mild but distinctive flavor. It is made with dried oregano, thyme, sesame seeds, and often sumac. You probably won't find it at your general supermarket, but you can order it through Amazon or find it at Middle Eastern spice shops. I love putting za'atar on everything from roast chicken to potatoes to crispy chickpea snacks. It adds a nice light spice and color to challah as well.

Yields 2 medium loaves

INGREDIENTS

FOR THE DOUGH:

1½ tablespoons dry active yeast

½ cup + 2 tablespoons + ½ teaspoon sugar

1¼ cups lukewarm water

4½–5 cups unbleached bread flour (preferably King Arthur)

1½ teaspoons table salt

¼ cup vegetable oil

2 tablespoons za'atar

½ teaspoon sumac

2 teaspoons jarred minced garlic in oil

2 large eggs

FOR THE TOPPING:

2 egg yolks (or 1 whole egg)

1 teaspoon water

1–2 teaspoons za'atar

¼ teaspoon sumac

¼ teaspoon coarse sea salt

INSTRUCTIONS

For the dough: In a small bowl, place the yeast, ½ teaspoon sugar, and lukewarm water. Stir gently to mix. Allow to sit 5 to 10 minutes, until it becomes foamy on top.

In a large bowl or stand mixer fitted with the whisk attachment, mix together 1½ cups of the flour, salt, and ½ cup plus 2 tablespoons sugar. Add the water-yeast mixture, oil, 2 tablespoons za'atar, sumac, and minced garlic to flour. Mix thoroughly.

Add another 1 cup of the flour and eggs and mix until smooth. Switch to the dough hook attachment if you are using a stand mixer. Add another 1½ to 2 cups of the flour and mix thoroughly. Remove from bowl and place on a floured surface. Knead the remaining ½ cup flour into dough, continuing to knead for about 5 minutes.

Place dough in a greased bowl and cover with a damp towel. Allow to rise at least 3 hours.

Divide the dough in two and braid the challahs into desired shape. See pages 32–45 for braiding.

Place braided challah on a baking sheet lined with parchment paper or silicone baking mat. Allow the challah to rise another 45 to 60 minutes, or until you can see the size has grown and the challah seems light. This step is very important to ensure a light and fluffy challah. Preheat oven to 375°F while the dough rises.

For the topping: In a small bowl beat 2 egg yolks with 1 teaspoon water. Brush the egg wash liberally over the challah. Sprinkle with za'atar, sumac, and coarse sea salt.

Bake 24 to 26 minutes, or until the color is golden.

HORSERADISH AND DILL CHALLAH

If you think horseradish is far too spicy for challah, think again. The horseradish in this recipe adds a nice tang that's just right. I love the smell and taste of the dill with the horseradish, but if you like some extra spice, add minced garlic and some red pepper flakes as a topping as well. But please note, this challah is best when served with cold vodka and pickles on the side.

Yields 2 medium loaves

INGREDIENTS

FOR THE DOUGH:

1½ tablespoons dry active yeast

½ cup + 2 tablespoons + ½ teaspoon sugar

1¼ cups lukewarm water

4½–5 cups unbleached bread flour (preferably King Arthur), + additional 1–2 tablespoons, if needed

1½ teaspoons table salt

¼ cup vegetable oil

1 tablespoon dried dill

⅓ cup prepared coarse horseradish

2 large eggs

INSTRUCTIONS

For the dough: In a small bowl, place the yeast, ½ teaspoon sugar, and lukewarm water. Stir gently to mix. Allow to sit 5 to 10 minutes, until it becomes foamy on top.

In a large bowl or stand mixer fitted with the whisk attachment, mix together 1½ cups of the flour, salt, and ½ cup plus 2 tablespoons sugar. Add the water-yeast mixture, oil, 1 tablespoon dill, and horseradish to the flour. Mix thoroughly.

Add another 1 cup of the flour and 2 eggs and mix until smooth. Switch to the dough hook attachment if you are using a stand mixer.

Add another 1½ to 2 cups of the flour and mix thoroughly. Remove from the bowl and place on a floured surface. Knead the remaining ½ cup flour into the dough, continuing to knead for about 5 minutes. You may need an additional 1 to 2 tablespoons flour if dough seems too sticky after kneading.

Place dough in a greased bowl and cover with a damp towel. Allow to rise at least 3 hours.

Divide the dough in two and braid the challahs into desired shape. See pages 32–45 for braiding.

Place braided challah on a baking sheet lined with parchment paper or silicone baking mat. Allow the challah to rise another 45 to 60 minutes, or until you can see the size has grown and challah seems light. This step is very important to ensure a light and fluffy challah. Preheat oven to 375°F while the dough rises.

continued

FOR THE TOPPING:

2 egg yolks (or 1 whole egg)

1 teaspoon water

½ teaspoon dried dill

1 teaspoon dried garlic flakes
(optional)

Pinch red pepper flakes
(optional)

¼ teaspoon coarse sea salt

For the topping: In a small bowl beat 2 egg yolks with
1 teaspoon water. Brush the egg wash liberally over the challah.
Sprinkle with additional dried dill, garlic flakes, red pepper
flakes, and coarse sea salt.

Bake 24 to 26 minutes, or until the color is golden.

TOMATO BASIL CHALLAH

I am always looking for ways to infuse some Italian-ness into my Jewish cooking, and a tomato basil challah is an obvious choice and a delicious pairing. The tomato paste adds both a beautiful red hue and a touch of sweetness to the dough. You can substitute with puréed sun-dried tomatoes or sun-dried tomato paste if you prefer.

Yields 2 medium loaves

INGREDIENTS

FOR THE DOUGH:

1½ tablespoons dry active yeast

½ cup + 2 tablespoons + ½ teaspoon sugar

1¼ cups lukewarm water

4½–5 cups unbleached bread flour (preferably King Arthur)

1½ teaspoons table salt

¼ cup vegetable oil

¼ cup tomato paste

2 teaspoons dried basil

2 large eggs

FOR THE TOPPING:

2 egg yolks (or 1 whole egg)

1 teaspoon water

1 teaspoon dried basil

¼ teaspoon coarse sea salt

INSTRUCTIONS

For the dough: In a small bowl, place the yeast, ½ teaspoon sugar, and lukewarm water. Stir gently to mix. Allow to sit 5 to 10 minutes, until it becomes foamy on top.

In a large bowl or stand mixer fitted with the whisk attachment, mix together 1½ cups of the flour, salt, and ½ cup plus 2 tablespoons sugar. Add the water-yeast mixture, oil, tomato paste, and 2 teaspoons dried basil to the flour. Mix thoroughly.

Add another 1 cup of the flour and 2 eggs and mix until smooth. Switch to the dough hook attachment if you are using a stand mixer.

Add another 1½ to 2 cups of the flour and mix thoroughly. Remove from the bowl and place on a floured surface. Knead the remaining ½ cup flour into the dough, continuing to knead for about 5 minutes.

Place dough in a greased bowl and cover with a damp towel. Allow to rise at least 3 hours.

Divide the dough in two and braid the challahs into desired shape. See pages 32–45 for braiding.

Place braided challah on a baking sheet lined with parchment paper or silicone baking mat. Allow challah to rise another 45 to 60 minutes, or until you can see the size has grown and challah seems light. This step is very important to ensure a light and fluffy challah. Preheat oven to 375°F while the dough rises.

For the topping: In a small bowl beat 2 egg yolks with 1 teaspoon water. Brush the egg wash liberally over the challah. Sprinkle with dried basil and coarse sea salt.

Bake 24 to 26 minutes, or until the color is golden.

CINNAMON RAISIN CHALLAH

Cinnamon raisin challah is a year-round classic, but it's especially perfect for Rosh Hashanah, the Jewish New Year, when it is practically a mitzvah to serve up sweet foods and breads to usher in a sweet year. If raisins aren't your thing, swap out the raisins for dark or semi-sweet chocolate chips. This recipe also makes wonderful French toast or bread pudding, that is *if* you have leftovers.

Yields 2 medium loaves

INGREDIENTS

FOR THE DOUGH:

1½ tablespoons dry active yeast

½ cup + 2 tablespoons + ½ teaspoon sugar

1¼ cups lukewarm water

4½–5 cups unbleached bread flour (preferably King Arthur)

1½ teaspoons table salt

¼ cup vegetable oil

2 teaspoons vanilla

1½ teaspoons cinnamon

2 large eggs

1 cup raisins

FOR THE TOPPING:

2 egg yolks (or 1 whole egg)

1 teaspoon water

¼ cup Spiced Sugar (page 16)

¼ teaspoon coarse sea salt

INSTRUCTIONS

For the dough: In a small bowl, place the yeast, ½ teaspoon sugar, and lukewarm water. Stir gently to mix. Allow to sit 5 to 10 minutes, until it becomes foamy on top.

In a large bowl or stand mixer fitted with the whisk attachment, mix together 1½ cups of the flour, salt, and ½ cup plus 2 tablespoons sugar. Add the water-yeast mixture, oil, vanilla, and cinnamon to the flour. Mix thoroughly.

Add another 1 cup of the flour and 2 eggs and mix until smooth. Switch to the dough hook attachment if you are using a stand mixer.

Add another 1½ to 2 cups of the flour and mix thoroughly. Remove from the bowl and place on a floured surface. Knead the remaining ½ cup flour into the dough, continuing to knead for about 5 minutes. Add the raisins and incorporate them into the kneaded dough.

Place dough in a greased bowl and cover with a damp towel. Allow to rise at least 3 hours.

Divide the dough in two and braid the challahs into desired shape. See pages 32–45 for braiding.

Place braided challah on a baking sheet lined with parchment paper or silicone baking mat. Allow the challah to rise another 45 to 60 minutes, or until you can see the size has grown and the challah seems light. This step is very important to ensure a light and fluffy challah. Preheat oven to 375°F while the dough rises.

For the topping: In a small bowl beat 2 egg yolks with 1 teaspoon water. Brush the egg wash liberally over the challah. Sprinkle with Spiced Sugar and coarse sea salt.

Bake 24 to 26 minutes, or until the color is golden.

WALNUT CRANBERRY RAISIN CHALLAH

Cinnamon raisin may be the most classic sweet challah flavor, and by adding walnuts, dried cranberries, and golden raisins, you have a sweet challah packed with heart-healthy nuts and lots of fun texture. It's delicious for Shabbat, but it's perhaps even more enjoyable for breakfast with some salted European butter.

Yields 2 medium loaves

INGREDIENTS

FOR THE DOUGH:

1½ tablespoons dry active yeast

½ cup + 2 tablespoons + ½ teaspoon sugar

1¼ cups lukewarm water

1 cup whole-wheat bread flour

3½–4 cups unbleached bread flour (preferably King Arthur)

1½ teaspoons table salt

¼ cup vegetable oil

2 teaspoons vanilla

1½ teaspoons cinnamon

2 large eggs

½ cup golden raisins

½ cup dried cranberries

½ cup coarsely chopped walnuts

INSTRUCTIONS

For the dough: In a small bowl, place the yeast, ½ teaspoon sugar, and lukewarm water. Stir gently to mix. Allow to sit 5 to 10 minutes, until it becomes foamy on top.

In a separate bowl, combine the wheat and white flours.

In a large bowl or stand mixer fitted with the whisk attachment, mix together 1½ cups of the mixed flours, salt, and ½ cup plus 2 tablespoons sugar. Add the water-yeast mixture, oil, vanilla, and cinnamon to the flour. Mix thoroughly.

Add another cup of the mixed flour and 2 eggs and mix until smooth. Switch to the dough hook attachment if you are using a stand mixer.

Add another 1½ to 2 cups of the flour and mix thoroughly. Remove from the bowl and place on a floured surface. Knead the remaining ½ cup flour into the dough for 1 minute. Add the raisins, dried cranberries, and walnuts, and continue to knead for about 4 minutes.

Place dough in a greased bowl and cover with a damp towel. Allow to rise at least 3 hours.

Divide the dough in two and braid the challahs into desired shape. See pages 32–45 for braiding.

Place braided challah on a baking sheet lined with parchment paper or silicone baking mat.

FOR THE TOPPING:

2 egg yolks (or 1 whole egg)

1 teaspoon water

2–3 tablespoons Spiced Sugar (page 16)

¼ teaspoon coarse sea salt

2–3 tablespoons oats (optional)

1 tablespoon flaxseed (optional)

2–3 tablespoons sunflower seeds (optional)

2–3 tablespoons chopped walnuts (optional)

Allow the challah to rise another 45 to 60 minutes, or until you can see the size has grown and the challah seems light. This step is very important to ensure a light and fluffy challah. Preheat oven to 375°F while the dough rises.

For the topping: In a small bowl beat 2 egg yolks with 1 teaspoon water. Brush the egg wash liberally over the challah. Sprinkle with Spiced Sugar and coarse sea salt. Alternatively, you can sprinkle with oats, flaxseed, sunflower seeds, and chopped walnuts.

Bake 24 to 26 minutes, or until the color is golden.

BANANA BREAD CHOCOLATE CHIP CHALLAH

The single item I remember baking the most with my mother was banana bread. I still have her copy of *Beard on Bread* and make the same recipe to this day. This challah recipe is a hybrid of that classic recipe. As a general note, when you add fresh fruit or vegetables (banana, apple, potato, squash, sweet potato, or pumpkin) you will always add more flour since fruit and vegetables release more water.

Yields 2 large loaves

INGREDIENTS

FOR THE DOUGH:

1½ tablespoons dry active yeast

½ cup + 2 tablespoons + ½ teaspoon sugar

1¼ cups lukewarm water

6½–7 cups unbleached bread flour (preferably King Arthur)

1½ teaspoons salt

¼ cup vegetable oil

2 teaspoons vanilla

½ teaspoon cinnamon

¼ cup whole or 2% milk (or almond milk)

½ teaspoon vinegar

2 mushy bananas, smashed

2 large eggs

1 cup semi-sweet or milk chocolate chips

INSTRUCTIONS

For the dough: In a small bowl, place the yeast, ½ teaspoon sugar, and lukewarm water. Stir gently to mix. Allow to sit 5 to 10 minutes, until it becomes foamy on top.

In a large bowl or stand mixer fitted with the whisk attachment, mix together 1½ cups of the flour, salt, and ½ cup plus 2 tablespoons sugar. Add the water-yeast mixture, oil, vanilla, and cinnamon to flour. Mix thoroughly.

In a separate small bowl combine the milk and vinegar. Allow to sit for 1 minute until curdled. Add the smashed bananas and 2 eggs.

Alternate adding 2 more cups of the flour and the banana-egg mixture to the dough. Switch to the dough hook if using a stand mixer.

Add another 2 cups of the flour and mix thoroughly. Add the remaining 1 to 1½ cups flour and chocolate chips until combined and dough is almost smooth. Then remove from the bowl and place on a lightly floured surface. Knead for 5 minutes.

Place dough in a greased bowl and cover with a damp towel. Allow to rise 3 hours.

Divide the dough in two and braid the challahs into desired shape. See pages 32–45 for braiding.

Place braided challah on a baking sheet lined with parchment paper or silicone baking mat.

continued

FOR THE TOPPING:

2 egg yolks

1 teaspoon water

¼ cup Spiced Sugar (page 16)

¼ teaspoon coarse sea salt

Allow the challah to rise another 45 to 60 minutes, or until you can see the size has grown and the challah seems light. Preheat oven to 375°F while the dough rises.

For the topping: In a small bowl beat 2 egg yolks with 1 teaspoon water. Brush the egg wash liberally over the challah. Sprinkle with Spiced Sugar and coarse sea salt.

Bake 24 to 26 minutes, or until the color is golden.

CHOCOLATE CHERRY CHALLAH

Dried cherries are one of my favorite ingredients to throw into muffins, salads, and challah. Tart, just a tad sweet, and packed with antioxidants, they are a slightly unexpected bite that perfectly accompanies sweet chocolate.

Yields 2 medium loaves

INGREDIENTS

FOR THE DOUGH:

1½ tablespoons dry active yeast

½ cup + 2 tablespoons + ½ teaspoon sugar

1¼ cups lukewarm water

4½–5 cups unbleached bread flour (preferably King Arthur)

1½ teaspoons table salt

¼ cup vegetable oil

2 teaspoons vanilla

1½ teaspoons cinnamon

2 large eggs

¾ cup chocolate chips

½ cup dried cherries

FOR THE TOPPING:

2 egg yolks (or 1 whole egg)

1 teaspoon water

¼ cup Spiced Sugar (page 16)

¼ teaspoon coarse sea salt

INSTRUCTIONS

For the dough: In a small bowl, place the yeast, ½ teaspoon sugar, and lukewarm water. Stir gently to mix. Allow to sit 5 to 10 minutes, until it becomes foamy on top.

In a large bowl or stand mixer fitted with the whisk attachment, mix together 1½ cups of the flour, salt, and ½ cup plus 2 tablespoons sugar. Add the water-yeast mixture, oil, vanilla, and cinnamon to the flour. Mix thoroughly.

Add another 1 cup of the flour and 2 eggs and mix until smooth. Switch to the dough hook attachment if you are using a stand mixer.

Add another 1½ to 2 cups of the flour and mix thoroughly. Remove from the bowl and place on a floured surface. Knead the remaining ½ cup flour into the dough, continuing to knead for about 5 minutes. While kneading, add the chocolate chips and dried cherries and incorporate into the dough.

Place dough in a greased bowl and cover with a damp towel. Allow to rise at least 3 hours.

Divide the dough in two and braid the challahs into desired shape. See pages 32–45 for braiding.

Place braided challah on a baking sheet lined with parchment paper or silicone baking mat. Allow the challah to rise another 45 to 60 minutes, or until you can see the size has grown and the challah seems light. This step is very important to ensure a light and fluffy challah. Preheat oven to 375°F while the dough rises.

For the topping: In a small bowl beat 2 egg yolks with 1 teaspoon water. Brush the egg wash liberally over the challah. Sprinkle with Spiced Sugar and coarse sea salt.

Bake 24 to 26 minutes, or until the color is golden.

BALSAMIC APPLE DATE STUFFED CHALLAH

This recipe was the first stuffed challah I ever created. It is a somewhat elevated version of a cinnamon raisin challah, but the dates and balsamic vinegar add a more sophisticated touch. Be warned: The smell of this challah as it bakes is absolutely intoxicating.

Yields 2 medium loaves

INGREDIENTS

FOR THE DOUGH:

1½ tablespoons dry active yeast

½ cup + 2 tablespoons + ½ teaspoon sugar

1¼ cups lukewarm water

4½–5 cups unbleached bread flour (preferably King Arthur)

1½ teaspoons table salt

2 teaspoons vanilla

1 teaspoon cinnamon

¼ teaspoon nutmeg

¼ cup vegetable oil

2 large eggs

FOR THE FILLING:

4 apples, peeled and diced

1 cup pitted dates, chopped

½ teaspoon salt

1 cinnamon stick

¾ cup water

¼ cup red wine

¼ cup white sugar

2 tablespoons balsamic vinegar

INSTRUCTIONS

For the dough: In a small bowl, place the yeast, ½ teaspoon sugar, and lukewarm water. Stir gently to mix. Allow to sit 5 to 10 minutes until it becomes foamy on top.

In a large bowl or stand mixer fitted with whisk attachment, mix together 1½ cups of the flour, salt, ½ cup plus 2 tablespoons sugar, vanilla, cinnamon, and nutmeg. Add the water-yeast mixture and oil to flour. Mix thoroughly.

Add another 1 cup of the flour and 2 eggs and mix until smooth. Switch to the dough hook attachment if you are using a stand mixer.

Add another 1½ to 2 cups cups of the flour and mix thoroughly. Remove from the bowl and place on a floured surface. Knead the remaining ½ cup flour into the dough, continuing to knead for about 5 minutes.

Place dough in a greased bowl and cover with a damp towel. Allow to rise 3 to 4 hours.

To make the filling, place the apples, dates, salt, cinnamon stick, water, red wine, and ¼ cup sugar in a medium saucepan and bring to a boil. Continue to simmer on medium heat until the mixture is reduced. Add the balsamic vinegar and simmer another 2 to 3 minutes. The mixture will cook 10 to 15 minutes in total.

Remove from the heat and allow to cool 5 minutes. Remove the cinnamon stick.

FOR THE TOPPING:

2 egg yolks (or 1 whole egg)

1 teaspoon water

¼ cup Spiced Sugar (page 16)

¼ teaspoon coarse sea salt

Place the mixture in a food processor fitted with a blade attachment and pulse until smooth. The consistency should resemble a thick, spreadable jam.

After the challah is done rising, cut the dough in half. To be as precise as possible, use a scale to measure the weight.

Roll out the first ball into approximately a large rectangle using a rolling pin. Spread about half, perhaps slightly less, of the apple-date mixture in an even layer, leaving a ½-inch border all around. Working quickly, roll the dough from the longer end toward you. Try to keep the roll relatively tight as you go. Pinch the ends when you finish.

Create a turban-shaped challah (pages 44–45) by snaking the dough around and around in a circle around itself. When finished, tuck the end under the challah neatly and pinch lightly. This doesn't have to be perfect.

Repeat with the other half of the dough. Place challahs on a baking sheet lined with parchment paper or a silicone baking mat.

Allow challahs to rise another 30 to 45 minutes, or until you can see the size has grown and dough seems light. Preheat oven to 375°F while the dough rises.

For the topping: Beat 2 egg yolks with 1 teaspoon water. Brush liberally over each challah. Top with Spiced Sugar and coarse sea salt.

Bake for 24 to 26 minutes, or until middle looks like it has just set, and the color is golden.

This recipe originally appeared on the blog The Nosher.

PUMPKIN SPICE CHALLAH

People have some strong feelings about pumpkin spice: some love it, some loathe it. Once September arrives, I want to put cinnamon, clove, and pumpkin in just about everything, including challah. Once this challah bakes up, your kitchen will smell like pure autumnal heaven. If by some chance you have leftovers, it makes wonderful French toast or indulgent White Chocolate Challah Bread Pudding (page 75).

Yields 2 medium loaves

INGREDIENTS

FOR THE DOUGH:

1½ tablespoons yeast

¾ cup + 1 teaspoon sugar

1¼ cups lukewarm water

5½–6 cups unbleached all-purpose flour (preferably King Arthur)

½ tablespoon salt

1 tablespoon cinnamon

1 teaspoon ground ginger

½ teaspoon ground nutmeg

½ teaspoon ground clove

¼ cup vegetable oil

2 teaspoons vanilla extract

½ cup canned or puréed pumpkin

2 eggs

INSTRUCTIONS

For the dough: In a small bowl, place the yeast, 1 teaspoon sugar, and lukewarm water. Stir gently to mix. Allow to sit about 10 minutes, until it becomes foamy on top.

In a large bowl or stand mixer fitted with the whisk attachment, mix together 1½ cups of the flour, salt, ¾ cup sugar, cinnamon, ginger, nutmeg, and clove. After the water-yeast mixture has become foamy, add to the flour mixture along with the oil, vanilla, and pumpkin. Mix thoroughly.

Add another 1 cup of the flour and 2 eggs and mix until smooth. Switch to the dough hook attachment if you are using a stand mixer.

Add another 2 cups of the flour and mix thoroughly. Remove from the bowl and place on a floured surface. Knead the remaining 1 to 1½ cups flour into the dough, continuing to knead for about 5 minutes. If the dough seems too soft, add ¼ to ½ cup flour until it is firmer.

Place dough in a greased bowl and cover with a damp towel. Allow to rise 3 hours.

Divide the dough in two and braid the challahs into desired shape. See pages 32–45 for braiding.

Place braided challah on a baking sheet lined with parchment paper or silicone baking mat. Allow the challah to rise another 30 to 60 minutes, or until you can see the size has grown and the challah seems light. Preheat oven to 375°F while the dough rises.

FOR THE TOPPING:

2 egg yolks

1 teaspoon water

¼ cup sugar

1 tablespoon cinnamon

¼–½ cup pepitas (pumpkin seeds)

1 teaspoon coarse sea salt (optional)

For the topping: In a small bowl beat 2 egg yolks with 1 teaspoon water. In another small bowl combine the ¼ cup sugar with 1 tablespoon cinnamon.

Brush the egg wash liberally over the challah. Sprinkle the pepitas in a single layer on top of the challah, followed by the cinnamon sugar and the coarse sea salt if desired.

Bake 24 to 26 minutes, or until the color is golden.

PESTO AND GOAT CHEESE STUFFED CHALLAH

Pesto is one of my favorite ingredients to stuff inside challah or babka. Because of the consistency of pesto, the flavors sort of infuse right into the dough as it bakes. Don't feel you have to restrict yourself to classic basil pesto—I have improvised various versions of pesto made from whatever is local and fresh at my farmers' market including kale, basil, spinach, garlic scapes, and even uber-trendy ramps. Note, this challah (as with all stuffed challahs) can either be made round (pages 44–45) or braided (pages 42–43).

Yields 2 medium loaves

INGREDIENTS

FOR THE DOUGH:

1½ tablespoons dry active yeast

½ cup + 2 tablespoons + ½ teaspoon sugar

1¼ cups lukewarm water

4½–5 cups unbleached bread flour (preferably King Arthur)

1½ teaspoons table salt

¼ cup vegetable oil

2 large eggs

INSTRUCTIONS

For the dough: In a small bowl, place the yeast, ½ teaspoon sugar, and lukewarm water. Stir gently to mix. Allow to sit 5 to 10 minutes, until it becomes foamy on top.

In a large bowl or stand mixer fitted with the whisk attachment, mix together 1½ cups of the flour, salt, and ½ cup plus 2 tablespoons sugar. Add the water-yeast mixture and oil to flour. Mix thoroughly.

Add another 1 cup of the flour and 2 eggs and mix until smooth. Switch to the dough hook attachment if you are using a stand mixer.

Add another 1½ to 2 cups of the flour and mix thoroughly. Remove from the bowl and place on a floured surface. Knead the remaining ½ cup flour into the dough, continuing to knead for about 5 minutes.

Place dough in a greased bowl and cover with a damp towel. Allow to rise at least 3 hours, punching down at least once if possible.

When fully risen, split the dough into two parts.

To make a braided stuffed challah (pages 42–43): Split each dough section into three additional sections. Roll each into a rope about 6 inches long. Flatten the ropes.

continued

FOR THE FILLING:

4 ounces pesto (store-bought or homemade)

6–8 ounces goat cheese (or feta)

FOR THE TOPPING:

2 egg yolks (or 1 beaten egg)

1 teaspoon water

1 teaspoon dried basil

¼ teaspoon coarse sea salt

Note: Some stuffing may pop out on the top or sides; this is fine. The round turban challah may require 1 to 2 additional minutes of baking to ensure it is cooked through inside.

Spread one-third of the pesto in the middle of each rope. Top each with one-third of the cheese. It may seem like a lot as you are doing it, and it will be messy, but the amount of filling can be deceiving.

Fold the sides of each rope up over the filling and pinch tightly. Roll slightly to even out the shape. Braid.

To make stuffed turban challah (pages 44–45): Roll out each of the two sections of dough into a large rectangle using a rolling pin. Spread about half of the pesto in an even layer on each rectangle, leaving a ½-inch border all around. Top each with half of the cheese.

Working quickly, roll each rectangle from the longer end into a long rope. Try to keep the roll relatively tight as you go. Pinch the ends when you finish. Circle the dough around itself and then pinch under.

Place challahs on a baking sheet lined with parchment paper or a silicone baking mat. Allow challah to rise another 30 to 45 minutes, or until you can see the size has grown and dough seems light. Preheat oven to 375°F while the dough rises.

For the topping: In a small bowl beat 2 egg yolks with 1 teaspoon water.

Brush the challah liberally with egg wash and top with dried basil and coarse sea salt. Bake for 24 to 26 minutes, or until golden brown.

LEFTOVER REMIX: WHITE CHOCOLATE CHALLAH BREAD PUDDING

This decadent bread pudding is perfect for a special breakfast-in-bed or dessert. You can use any challah you like in this recipe, but it is especially delicious with leftover pumpkin spice challah all autumn long. Serve with fresh whipped cream and a dash of cinnamon.

Yields 4 to 6 servings

INGREDIENTS

½ loaf leftover Challah cut into 1-inch cubes (about 4 ½ cups)

¼ cup (½ stick) unsalted butter, melted

1 cup white chocolate chips or chunks

3 large eggs

¾ cup heavy cream

¾ cup milk

⅓ cup sugar

½ teaspoon vanilla

½ teaspoon cinnamon

Vanilla ice cream, for serving (optional)

Whipped cream, for serving (optional)

INSTRUCTIONS

Preheat oven to 325°F. Grease an 8-inch square baking pan.

Place the cubed challah in the baking pan and drizzle with the melted butter. Toss with fingers to ensure bread is covered. Add white chocolate chips and mix.

In a large bowl, whisk the 3 eggs.

Place the heavy cream, milk, sugar, vanilla, and cinnamon in a medium saucepan over medium-high heat. Bring to a boil and then remove from heat.

Slowly stir the hot milk mixture into the eggs. Skim off any foam on top of surface. Strain the custard mixture over the bread and allow to sit for 10 minutes to allow custard to fully soak into the bread.

Place the pan with the bread pudding into another larger pan. Pour hot water into the larger pan until it reaches halfway up the pan. Don't fill with too much water, otherwise it could spill into the bread pudding.

Bake the bread pudding for 1 hour, until the custard is set and the top of the bread is golden. Serve warm with vanilla ice cream or whipped cream, if desired.

This recipe originally appeared in Joy of Kosher *magazine.*

CHALLAH DOGS AND PRETZEL CHALLAH DOGS

Challah wrapped hot dogs were one of my very first challah experiments, and from day one they were a huge hit. I make challah dogs for almost every party or family event. They are crowd-pleasing like pigs in blankets, but just a little more indulgent.

Pretzel dogs are a newer invention from my kitchen, and one that I am sure you will love. With only one additional step of boiling the prepared challah dogs, you turn your regular challah dough into something really special. The smell is intoxicating—like real soft pretzels. You can try this technique for any kind of challah, such as rolls or even a whole loaf.

I typically use an all-beef kosher hot dog, but there's no reason why you can't use turkey hot dogs, sausages, or even soy-based hot dogs.

Yields 14 challah dogs or pretzel challah dogs

INGREDIENTS

FOR THE DOUGH:

1½ tablespoons dry active yeast

¾ cup sugar + 1 teaspoon sugar

1¼ cups lukewarm water

4½–5 cups unbleached bread flour (preferably King Arthur)

½ tablespoon salt

¼ cup vegetable oil

2 eggs

14 kosher hot dogs

INSTRUCTIONS

For the dough: In a small bowl, place the yeast, 1 teaspoon sugar, and lukewarm water. Stir gently to mix. Allow to sit 5 to 10 minutes, until it becomes foamy on top.

In a large bowl or stand mixer fitted with the whisk attachment, mix together 1½ cups of the flour, salt, and ¾ cup sugar. Add the water-yeast mixture and oil to the flour. Mix thoroughly.

Add another 1 cup of the flour and 2 eggs and mix until smooth. Switch to the dough hook attachment if you are using a stand mixer.

Add another 1½ to 2 cups of flour and mix thoroughly. Remove from the bowl and place on a floured surface. Knead the remaining ½ cup flour into the dough, continuing to knead for about 5 minutes.

Place dough in a greased bowl and cover with a damp towel. Allow to rise at least 3 hours.

After the dough has risen, divide into 14 equal pieces, about 2½ ounces each (use a food scale for an exact measurement). Roll each piece of dough into a rope about 4 to 5 inches long.

Wrap the dough around each hot dog, pinching ends under and placing on a baking sheet lined with parchment paper or silicone baking mat.

continued

FOR THE PRETZEL CHALLAH VARIATION:

1 heaping teaspoon baking soda

Pinch table salt

Coarse sea salt

FOR THE TOPPING:

1 egg

1 teaspoon water

A few tablespoons of each: sesame seeds, poppy seeds, black sesame seeds, caraway seeds, and coarse sea salt (optional)

To make pretzel challah dogs, skip the next steps and see variation instructions below.

Allow to rise 15 to 20 minutes. Preheat oven to 375°F while the dough rises.

For the topping: Whisk 1 egg with 1 teaspoon water and brush each challah dog with egg wash. Top with sesame seeds, poppy seeds, black sesame seeds, caraway seeds, or coarse sea salt if desired.

Bake for 20 to 23 minutes, until golden brown on top. Serve warm with mustard or ketchup.

VARIATION: PRETZEL CHALLAH DOGS

Follow the previous directions for Challah Dogs until the challah dogs are formed, but haven't yet done a second rise.

Bring a large pot of water to boil. Add 1 heaping teaspoon baking soda and a pinch salt. Add each challah dog to the pot of water and let sit for 30 to 60 seconds, until puffed just slightly.

Remove from the water using a spider (a long-handled spoon with a fine-mesh basket) and allow excess water to drip back into the pot.

Place the challah dogs on a baking sheet lined with parchment paper or a silicone baking mat. Sprinkle with coarse sea salt on top.

Bake for 20 to 23 minutes or until deep brown and the kitchen smells like pretzels. Serve warm with mustard or ketchup.

ONION CHALLAH ROLLS

Individual challah rolls are the ideal vessel for serving pulled brisket sandwiches, piled-high pastrami, mozzarella, tomato, and homemade Gravlax (page 155) for Sunday brunch. Instead of dried onions on top, you can try topping with rosemary, Everything Bagel Topping (page 14), or just plain poppy seeds. Though my favorite combination are these onion rolls with classic, American Sloppy Joes (page 83).

Yields 10 to 12 rolls

INGREDIENTS

FOR THE DOUGH:

1½ tablespoons dry active yeast

½ cup sugar + ½ teaspoon sugar

1¼ cups lukewarm water

5 cups unbleached bread flour (preferably King Arthur), + more if needed

2 teaspoons onion powder

1½ teaspoons salt

¼ cup vegetable or olive oil

1 tablespoon jarred minced garlic in oil

2 eggs

FOR THE TOPPING:

2 egg yolks (or 1 whole egg)

1 teaspoon water

1–2 tablespoons minced, dried onion flakes

1 teaspoon coarse sea salt

INSTRUCTIONS

For the dough: In a small bowl place the yeast, ½ teaspoon sugar, and lukewarm water. Stir gently to mix. Allow to sit 5 to 10 minutes until it becomes foamy on top.

In a large bowl or stand mixer fitted with whisk attachment, mix together 1½ cups of the flour, ½ cup sugar, onion powder, and salt. Add the water-yeast mixture, oil, and garlic to the flour. Mix thoroughly.

Add another 1½ cups of the flour and 2 eggs and mix until smooth. Switch to the dough hook attachment if you are using a stand mixer. Add the remaining flour 1 cup at a time and let the mixer run until the dough is smooth and sticks just slightly. If not using a mixer, use a wooden spoon until the dough starts to come together, and then dump out onto a floured work surface. Knead the dough using the heel of your hand until dough is lump-free. Depending on humidity, time of year, and the flour you use, you may need slightly more or less flour. You can add 1 tablespoon at a time until desired consistency.

Place dough in a greased bowl and cover with a towel. Allow to rise 3 hours.

Remove dough from the bowl, punch down, and cut into 10 to 12 equal pieces, 3 to 3.5 ounces each (use a food scale for an exact measurement). Roll each section in a rope and shape into a knotted roll. See pages 40–41 for shaping. Place on a baking sheet lined with parchment paper or silicone baking mat. Allow challah rolls to rise another 20 to 30 minutes. Preheat oven to 375°F while the dough rises.

For the topping: Beat 2 egg yolks with 1 teaspoon water in a small bowl. Using a pastry brush, glaze the challah with two coatings of egg wash. Sprinkle with dried onion flakes and sea salt.

Bake for 25 minutes or until just golden on top and challah feels light and hollow. Cool on a wire baking rack.

HAVE WITH: SLOPPY JOE FILLING

I don't remember at what point I started serving sloppy joes on Onion Challah Rolls, but it is a winning combination that gets requested over and over again. You can also use the Everything Bagel Topping (page 14) and make everything challah rolls to go with sloppy joes, pulled brisket, hamburgers, or your favorite, messy sandwich. This isn't highbrow cooking, but it is fun and crowd-pleasing.

Yields 8 to 10 servings

INGREDIENTS

1–2 tablespoons olive oil

1 large onion, diced

1 garlic clove, minced

2 pounds ground beef

1 tablespoon tomato paste

1 cup ketchup

1 tablespoon brown sugar

2 tablespoons apple cider vinegar

1 teaspoon Dijon mustard

¼ teaspoon cinnamon

½ teaspoon paprika

Salt and pepper to taste

½ cup water or broth

Onion Challah Rolls (page 81), for serving

Pickle chips, for serving

INSTRUCTIONS

Heat the oil in a large pan over medium-high heat. Add the onion and sauté until soft and translucent, 3 to 5 minutes. Add the garlic clove and cook another 2 minutes. Add the ground beef and begin breaking up into small, even pieces using a wooden spoon. Once the meat is cooked through, create a small space in the middle and add the tomato paste. Cook 1 to 2 minutes.

In a small bowl combine the ketchup, brown sugar, apple cider vinegar, mustard, and spices. Mix well.

Add the ketchup mixture to the pan and combine. Add the water and bring to a boil. Reduce the heat to medium-low and cook 30 minutes uncovered.

Serve with Onion Challah Rolls and pickle chips.

PULL-APART CHALLAH WITH SPINACH ARTICHOKE DIP

Far from a classic loaf of challah served for Shabbat dinner, this appetizer is perfect for a game night with friends, a cocktail party, or Super Bowl viewing. No forks or plates required; just use your hands and dig in. I like to alternate the toppings on the challah balls to make a beautiful pattern: sesame seeds, dried garlic, poppy seeds, or dried herbs would be my suggestions. If you have a different spinach artichoke dip you love using, no reason not to swap it in.

Yields 2 pull-apart rounds

INGREDIENTS

FOR THE DOUGH:

1½ tablespoons dry active yeast

½ cup + 2 tablespoons + ½ teaspoon sugar

1¼ cups lukewarm water

4½–5 cups unbleached bread flour (preferably King Arthur)

1½ teaspoons table salt

¼ cup vegetable oil

2 large eggs

INSTRUCTIONS

For the dough: In a small bowl, place the yeast, ½ teaspoon sugar, and lukewarm water. Stir gently to mix. Allow to sit 5 to 10 minutes, until it becomes foamy on top.

In a large bowl or stand mixer fitted with the whisk attachment, mix together 1½ cups of the flour, salt, and ½ cup plus 2 tablespoons sugar. Add the water-yeast mixture and oil to flour. Mix thoroughly.

Add another 1 cup of the flour and 2 eggs and mix until smooth. Switch to the dough hook attachment if you are using a stand mixer.

Add another 1½ to 2 cups of the flour and mix thoroughly. Remove from the bowl and place on a floured surface. Knead the remaining ½ cup flour into the dough, continuing to knead for about 5 minutes.

Place dough in a greased bowl and cover with a damp towel. Allow to rise at least 3 hours, punching down at least once if possible.

continued

FOR THE DIP:

12 ounces frozen artichokes, thawed and chopped

8 ounces frozen spinach, thawed and drained

6 ounces whole milk Greek yogurt or sour cream

1 cup shredded Cheddar

4 ounces cream cheese, at room temperature

2 ounces goat cheese, at room temperature

¼ cup grated Parmesan + more for topping, if desired

2 teaspoons Worcestershire sauce

½ teaspoon salt

¼ teaspoon pepper

Pinch red pepper flakes

FOR THE TOPPING:

1 egg, beaten

1 teaspoon water

1–2 teaspoons dried herbs such as basil, oregano, or parsley

1–2 teaspoons sesame seeds

¼ teaspoon coarse sea salt

For the dip: While the dough is rising, prepare the artichoke dip. Combine all the ingredients in a large bowl. Set aside.

Grease two 8- or 9-inch round cake pans. You can also use a cast iron skillet.

After the dough has risen 3 hours, divide dough into two equal parts.

Divide each part into 10 to 12 even-sized pieces (use a food scale to measure exactly). Roll each piece into a ball. Place challah balls around outside of cake pan. Repeat with second part of dough. Allow to rise 30 minutes. Preheat oven to 375°F while the dough rises.

Divide the dip into equal parts. Spoon the dip into the middle of each pan.

For the topping: In a small bowl, beat 2 egg yolks with 1 teaspoon water. Brush the challah with egg wash. Sprinkle with dried herbs, sesame seeds, and/or coarse sea salt.

Bake for 23 to 25 minutes, until the challah is golden and artichoke dip is gooey and melted. Top with additional grated Parmesan, if desired.

BABKA

Babka, like rugelach, is a classic Eastern European cake made from a yeasted dough and iconic layers of chocolate or cinnamon filling. In Israeli it is called kranz cake, *kranz* being German for crown. Until fairly recently, babka was almost a forgotten Jewish dessert. You could buy it in kosher shops or packaged from the gourmet shop Zabar's in New York City, but it was hardly the star of the dessert spread. It is only in the past few years, particularly since the emergence of Breads Bakery in New York City, that babka achieved rockstar status.

These days babka has taken on a life of its own—coveted by foodies, reinterpreted by chefs and bloggers all over the United States. I have seen every variety of babka from sweet matcha and black sesame babka to savory pulled brisket babka. Babka can seem daunting—how do you achieve those swirls? But once you know how simple it is to make, you will be experimenting with sweet and savory flavor combinations of your own.

HOW THE DOUGH SHOULD FEEL

Babka dough will be the lightest of the yeasted doughs in this book. It should be very shiny and elastic with a luxurious texture and sheen.

RISING

The babka dough should only rise 1 to 2 hours at most. I do not recommend making babka dough ahead of time and allowing to rise in the fridge.

STORAGE

The dough recipe will yield 3 medium-sized babkas, or 2 larger babkas. Allow to cool completely before storing in a sealable plastic bag. You can wrap babka in tin foil, then place in freezer bag and store for up to 2 months. Defrost and warm slightly to serve.

FLOUR

You can use an unbleached all-purpose flour for babka.

ESSENTIAL TOOLS

You may want to invest in three 8½-by-4½-inch *loaf pans*, as this recipe yields three medium babkas. You can also make one loaf and two rounds, or one loaf and one larger round.

A good *dough cutter* is necessary for splitting the babka dough to create those coveted swirls.

Using your *food scale* is also useful in babka. When you split the dough between pans, whether in half or thirds, use your food scale to measure the amount of dough.

Make sure to have a *wooden pastry brush* for those babka recipes that call for sugar syrup.

SPECIAL NOTES

I recommend adding a sugar syrup on top of sweet babkas both while baking and immediately when the babka emerges from the oven. This step is omitted with savory babkas.

Making babka can be quite messy, so be prepared to get your hands and your counters dirty. You want your fillings, whether sweet or savory, to be on the gooier side to ensure a moist babka packed with swirls of flavors.

SHAPING BABKA

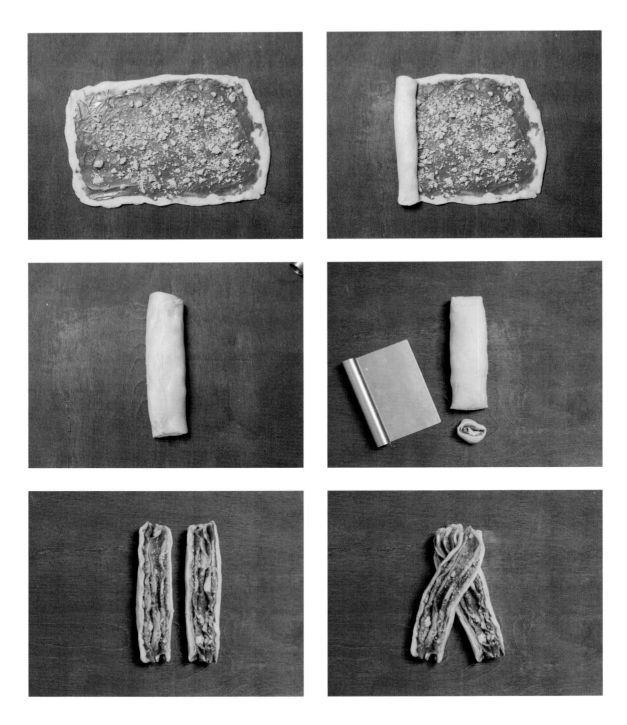

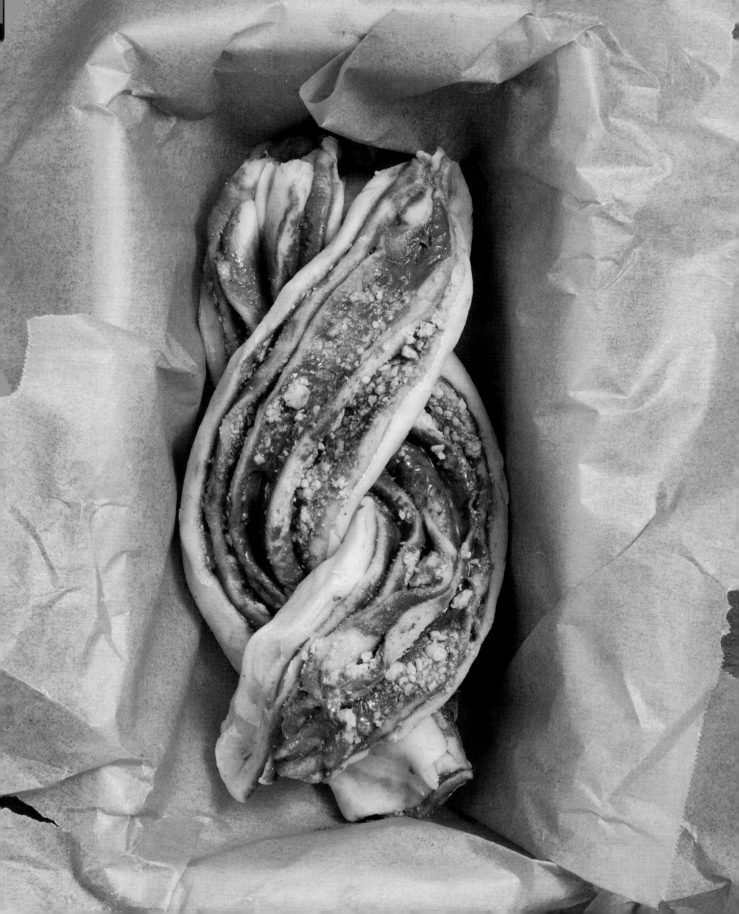

SHAPING ROUND BABKA

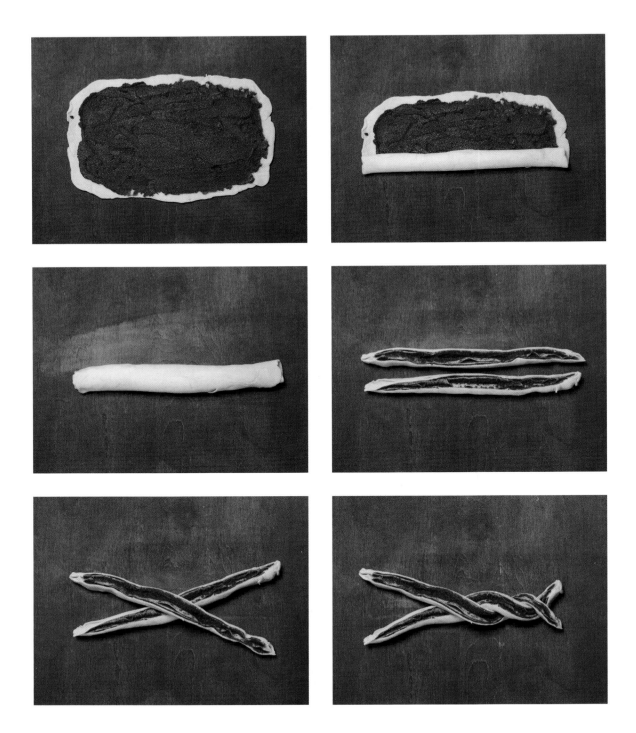

BASIC SWEET BABKA

I was always intimidated to make babka because of those coveted swirls. But once I bit the bullet and saw how similar babka dough is to challah, I realized the task was far more realistic than I'd thought. This sweet babka dough is more elastic, smoother, and shinier than challah dough. You want to roll it out as thinly as possible on a lightly floured surface to achieve as many of those beautiful and delicious swirls as possible.

Yields 3 loaves

INGREDIENTS

FOR THE DOUGH:

1 tablespoon dry active yeast

⅓ cup + ½ teaspoon sugar

½ cup lukewarm water

4½ cups unbleached all-purpose flour

2 teaspoons vanilla

½ cup whole or 2% milk (or almond milk)

¾ cup (1½ sticks) unsalted butter (or margarine), melted

2 eggs

SUGGESTED FILLINGS:

1–1½ cups Chocolate Filling (page 26), Cinnamon Sugar (page 25), or other filling of your choice

FOR THE SUGAR SYRUP:

⅔ cup water

1 cup sugar

1 teaspoon vanilla

INSTRUCTIONS

For the dough: Place the yeast and ½ teaspoon sugar in a small bowl. Add the lukewarm water and stir gently to mix. Set aside until foamy, 5 to 10 minutes.

In a stand mixer fitted with a dough hook, mix together the flour, ⅓ cup sugar, and 2 teaspoons vanilla.

In a medium saucepan, scald the milk (bring almost to a boil, until milk is just simmering). Allow to sit for 1 minute to cool just slightly.

With mixer on low, add the water-yeast mixture, milk, and melted butter. Add the eggs one at a time.

When the dough begins to come together, after 2 to 3 minutes, turn off the mixer and scrape down the sides. Raise the speed to high and mix for another 5 to 10 minutes until the dough is shiny, elastic, and smooth. It may seem like a long time to mix, but the result is worth the wait.

Place dough in a greased bowl with a damp towel on top. Allow to rise 1 to 2 hours.

Make the sugar syrup while the dough is rising: Combine the water, sugar, and vanilla in a small saucepan. Bring to a low boil until the sugar has dissolved. Set aside and cool. This syrup can be kept in the fridge for 2 to 3 months and makes enough for at least 2 batches of babka (6 medium babkas).

Prepare three 8½-by-4½-inch greased loaf pans. Note: you can also make two larger round babkas that can be baked on baking sheets.

continued

Cut the dough into three equal parts (use a food scale for precision). Roll out one part into a rectangle. Spread one-third of the filling onto the rectangle and roll up along the shorter side (to create more swirls inside). See pages 92–93 for shaping.

Once the dough is formed into a swirled log, cut it straight down the middle so the filling is exposed. Cut ½ inch off each end. Layer each cut piece on top of one another and twist. Place in a greased loaf pan.

Repeat with the other two pieces of babka dough. Lightly drape a kitchen towel over the top of the pans. Allow to rise another 30 minutes. Preheat oven to 350°F while the dough rises.

Bake for 20 minutes. Brush each babka with two layers of sugar syrup. Place back in the oven for approximately 15 minutes. The edges should be slightly brown and the middle should be slightly doughy.

When the babkas come out of the oven, immediately brush each with another 3 light layers of sugar syrup.

Allow to cool for 5 to 10 minutes. Using a butter knife, loosen the sides of the babka from the pan and place on top of wire rack to cool.

BASIC SAVORY BABKA

Savory babkas have been cropping up all over the place—from supermarkets to restaurants. Creating the savory babka dough is done using the same process as sweet babka, but without as much sugar, or vanilla.

Yields 3 loaves

INGREDIENTS

FOR THE DOUGH:

1 tablespoon dry active yeast

3 tablespoons + ½ teaspoon sugar

½ cup lukewarm water

4½ cups unbleached all-purpose flour

¼ teaspoon salt

½ cup whole or 2% milk (or almond milk)

¾ cup (1½ sticks) unsalted butter (or margarine), melted

2 eggs

SUGGESTED FILLINGS:

1–1½ cups Kale Basil Pesto (page 20), Savory Onion Jam (page 23), or other filling of your choice

FOR THE TOPPING:

1½ cups shredded Gruyère or mozzarella (if using pesto filling; optional)

3 ounces goat cheese, crumbled (if using onion filling; optional)

INSTRUCTIONS

For the dough: Place the yeast and ½ teaspoon sugar in a small bowl. Add the lukewarm water and stir gently to mix. Set aside until foamy, 5 to 10 minutes.

In a stand mixer fitted with a dough hook, mix together the flour, 3 tablespoons sugar, and salt.

In a medium saucepan, scald the milk (bring almost to a boil, until milk is just simmering). Allow to sit for 1 minute to cool just slightly.

With mixer on low, add the water-yeast mixture, milk, and melted butter. Add the eggs one at a time.

When the dough begins to come together, after 2 to 3 minutes, turn off the mixer and scrape down the sides. Raise the speed to high and mix for another 5 to 10 minutes until the dough is shiny, elastic, and smooth. It may seem like a long time to mix, but the result is worth the wait.

Prepare three 8½-by-4½-inch greased loaf pans. Note: you can also make two larger round babkas that can be baked on baking sheets.

Cut the dough into three equal parts (use a food scale for precision). Roll out one part into a rectangle. Spread one-third of the filling onto the rectangle and roll up along the shorter side (to create more swirls inside). See pages 92–93 for shaping.

Once the dough is formed into a swirled log, cut it straight down the middle so the filling is exposed. Cut ½ inch off each end. Layer each cut piece on top of one another and twist. Place in a greased loaf pan.

continued

Repeat with the other two pieces of babka dough. Lightly drape a kitchen towel over the top of pans. Allow to rise another 30 minutes. Preheat oven to 350°F while the dough rises.

Top each babka with one-third of the cheese, if using.

Bake for approximately 35 minutes. The edges should be slightly brown and the middle should be slightly doughy.

Allow to cool for 5 to 10 minutes. Using a butter knife, loosen sides of babka from the pan and place on top of wire rack to cool.

CHOCOLATE BABKA

The most classic flavor of babka is chocolate, and not just because it was Elaine Benes and Jerry Seinfeld's favorite. Rich chocolate, butter, and sugar get folded into layers of sweet dough for one of the most iconic Jewish desserts.

Yields 3 loaves

INGREDIENTS

FOR THE DOUGH:

1 tablespoon dry active yeast

⅓ cup + ½ teaspoon sugar

½ cup lukewarm water

4½ cups unbleached all-purpose flour

2 teaspoons vanilla

½ cup whole or 2% milk (or almond milk)

¾ cup (1½ sticks) unsalted butter (or margarine), melted

2 eggs

FOR THE SUGAR SYRUP:

⅔ cup water

1 cup sugar

1 teaspoon vanilla

FOR THE FILLING:

1 batch Chocolate Filling (page 26)

INSTRUCTIONS

For the dough: Place the yeast and ½ teaspoon sugar in a small bowl. Add the lukewarm water and stir gently to mix. Set aside until foamy, 5 to 10 minutes.

In a stand mixer fitted with a dough hook, mix together the flour, ⅓ cup sugar, and vanilla.

In a medium saucepan, scald the milk (bring almost to a boil, until milk is just simmering). Allow to sit for 1 minute to cool just slightly.

With mixer on low, add the water-yeast mixture, milk, and melted butter. Add the eggs one at a time.

When the dough begins to come together, after 2 to 3 minutes, turn off the mixer and scrape down the sides. Raise the speed to high and mix for another 5 to 10 minutes until the dough is shiny, elastic, and smooth. It may seem like a long time to mix, but the result is worth the wait.

Place dough in a greased bowl with a damp towel on top. Allow to rise 1 to 2 hours.

Make the sugar syrup while dough is rising. Combine water, sugar, and vanilla in a small saucepan. Bring to a low boil until the sugar has dissolved. Set aside and cool. This syrup can be kept in the fridge for 2 to 3 months and makes enough for at least 2 batches of babka (6 medium babkas).

Prepare three 8½-by-4½-inch greased loaf pans. Note: you can also make two larger round babkas that can be baked on baking sheets.

continued

Cut the dough into three equal parts (use a food scale for precision). Roll out one part into a rectangle. Spread with one-third of the filling and roll up along the shorter side (to create more swirls inside). See pages 92–93 for shaping.

Once the dough is formed into a swirled log, cut it straight down the middle so the filling is exposed. Cut ½ inch off each end. Layer each cut piece on top of one another and twist. Place in a greased loaf pan.

Repeat with the other two parts of babka dough. Lightly drape a kitchen towel over the top of pans. Allow to rise another 30 minutes. Preheat oven to 350°F while the dough rises.

Bake for 20 minutes. Brush each babka with two layers of sugar syrup. Place back in the oven for approximately 15 minutes. The edges should be slightly brown and the middle should be slightly doughy.

When the babkas come out of the oven, immediately brush each with another 3 light layers of sugar syrup.

Allow to cool for 5 to 10 minutes. Using a butter knife, loosen the sides of the babka from the pan and place on wire rack to cool.

CINNAMON BABKA

Cinnamon babka really gets a bad rap, but I think this version is just as delicious and decadent as its more popular cousin, the chocolate babka. If you want to add a little spice to this babka, add ¼ teaspoon ground clove and a pinch ground allspice to the filling mixture.

Yields 3 loaves

INGREDIENTS

FOR THE DOUGH:

1 tablespoon dry active yeast

⅓ cup + ½ teaspoon sugar

½ cup lukewarm water

4½ cups unbleached all-purpose flour

2 teaspoons vanilla

½ cup whole or 2% milk (or almond milk)

¾ cup (1½ sticks) unsalted butter (or margarine), melted

2 eggs

FOR THE SUGAR SYRUP:

⅔ cup water

1 cup sugar

1 teaspoon vanilla

FOR THE FILLING:

1 batch Cinnamon Sugar Filling (page 25)

INSTRUCTIONS

For the dough: Place the yeast and ½ teaspoon sugar in a small bowl. Add the lukewarm water and stir gently to mix. Set aside until foamy, 5 to 10 minutes.

In a stand mixer fitted with a dough hook, mix together the flour, ⅓ cup sugar, and 2 teaspoons vanilla.

In a medium saucepan, scald the milk (bring almost to a boil, until milk is just simmering). Allow to sit for 1 minute to cool just slightly.

With mixer on low, add the water-yeast mixture, milk, and melted butter. Add eggs one at a time.

When the dough begins to come together, after 2 to 3 minutes, turn off mixer and scrape down the sides. Raise the speed to high and mix for another 5 to 10 minutes until the dough is shiny, elastic, and smooth. It may seem like a long time to mix, but the result is worth the wait.

Place dough in a greased bowl with a damp towel on top. Allow to rise 1 to 2 hours.

Make the sugar syrup while dough is rising: Combine water, sugar, and vanilla in a small saucepan. Bring to a low boil until the sugar has dissolved. Set aside and cool. This syrup can be kept in the fridge for 2 to 3 months and makes enough for at least 2 batches of babka (6 medium babkas).

Prepare three 8½-by-4½-inch greased loaf pans. Note: you can also make two larger round babkas that can be baked on baking sheets.

continued

Cut the dough into three equal parts (use a food scale for precision). Roll out one part into a rectangle. Spread with one-third of the filling and roll up along the shorter side (to create more swirls inside). See pages 92–93 for shaping.

Once the dough is formed into a swirled log, cut it straight down the middle so the filling is exposed. Cut ½ inch off each end. Layer each cut piece on top of one another and twist. Place in a greased loaf pan.

Repeat with the other two pieces of babka dough. Lightly drape a kitchen towel over the top of pans. Allow to rise another 30 minutes. Preheat oven to 350°F while the dough rises.

Bake for 20 minutes. Brush each babka with two layers of sugar syrup. Place back in the oven for approximately 15 minutes. The edges should be slightly brown and the middle should be slightly doughy.

When the babkas come out of the oven, immediately brush each with another 3 light layers of sugar syrup.

Allow to cool for 5 to 10 minutes. Using a butter knife, loosen sides of the babka from the pan and place on wire rack to cool.

S'MORES BABKA

It has been said that I will try to "smorify" anything, and it's true—I love the simple, classic American flavors of sweet chocolate, gooey marshmallow, and crunchy graham crackers. The filling of this babka is a celebration in sweetness and texture, no campfire necessary.

Yields 3 loaves

INGREDIENTS

FOR THE DOUGH:

1 tablespoon dry active yeast

⅓ cup + ½ teaspoon sugar

½ cup lukewarm water

4½ cups unbleached all-purpose flour

2 teaspoons vanilla

½ cup whole or 2% milk (or almond milk)

¾ cup (1½ sticks) unsalted butter (or margarine), melted

2 eggs

FOR THE SUGAR SYRUP:

⅔ cup water

1 cup sugar

1 teaspoon vanilla

FOR THE FILLING:

⅓ cup chocolate hazelnut spread

½ cup marshmallow fluff

¼ cup crushed graham cracker crumbs

FOR THE TOPPING:

1 recipe Crumb Topping (page 19)

INSTRUCTIONS

For the dough: Place the yeast and ½ teaspoon sugar in a small bowl. Add the lukewarm water and stir gently to mix. Set aside until foamy, 5 to 10 minutes.

In a stand mixer fitted with a dough hook, mix together the flour, ⅓ cup sugar, and 2 teaspoons vanilla.

In a medium saucepan, scald the milk (bring almost to a boil, until milk is just simmering). Allow to sit for 1 minute to cool just slightly.

With mixer on low, add the water-yeast mixture, milk, and melted butter. Add eggs one at a time.

When the dough begins to come together, after 2 to 3 minutes, turn off mixer and scrape down the sides. Raise the speed to high and mix for another 5 to 10 minutes until the dough is shiny, elastic, and smooth. It may seem like a long time to mix, but the result is worth the wait.

Place dough in a greased bowl with a damp towel on top. Allow to rise 1 to 2 hours.

Make the sugar syrup while dough is rising: Combine water, sugar, and vanilla in a small saucepan. Bring to a low boil until sugar has dissolved. Set aside and cool. This syrup can be kept in the fridge for 2 to 3 months and makes enough for at least 2 batches of babka (6 medium babkas).

Prepare three 8½-by-4½-inch greased loaf pans. Note: you can also make two larger round babkas that can be baked on baking sheets.

continued

Cut the dough into three equal parts (use a food scale for precision). Roll out one part into a rectangle. Spread with one-third each of the chocolate hazelnut spread, then marshmallow fluff, and then sprinkle with graham cracker crumbs, and roll up along the shorter side (to create more swirls inside). See pages 92–93 for shaping.

Once the dough is formed into a swirled log, cut it straight down the middle so the filling is exposed. Cut ½ inch off each end. Layer each cut piece on top of one another and twist. Place in a greased loaf pan.

Repeat with the other two pieces of babka dough. Lightly drape a kitchen towel over the top of pans. Allow to rise another 30 minutes. Preheat oven to 375°F while the dough rises.

Top with Crumb Topping. Bake for 20 minutes. Brush each babka with two layers of sugar syrup. Place back in the oven for approximately 15 minutes. The edges should be slightly brown and the middle should be slightly doughy.

When the babkas come out of the oven, immediately brush each with another 3 light layers of sugar syrup.

Allow to cool for 5 to 10 minutes. Using a butter knife, loosen sides of the babka from the pan and place on wire rack to cool.

TROPICAL BABKA

I will admit, I was skeptical about creating a "tropical" inspired babka. After all, sweet babka stuffed with coconut and pineapple is kind of the antithesis of classic babka. But this recipe is creamy and crunchy, and the drizzle of white chocolate on top makes it look impressive and taste wonderful.

Yields 3 loaves

INGREDIENTS

FOR THE DOUGH:

1 tablespoon dry active yeast

⅓ cup + ½ teaspoon sugar

½ cup lukewarm water

4½ cups unbleached all-purpose flour

2 teaspoons vanilla

½ cup whole or 2% milk (or almond milk)

¾ cup (1½ sticks) unsalted butter (or margarine), melted

2 eggs

FOR THE SUGAR SYRUP:

⅔ cup water

1 cup sugar

1 teaspoon vanilla

FOR THE FILLING:

12 ounces cream cheese, softened

8 ounces canned crushed pineapple pieces (drained of excess juice)

1 cup shredded coconut

FOR THE TOPPING:

1 cup white chocolate chips

1 tablespoon vegetable oil

INSTRUCTIONS

For the dough: Place the yeast and ½ teaspoon sugar in a small bowl. Add the lukewarm water and stir gently to mix. Set aside until foamy, 5 to 10 minutes.

In a stand mixer fitted with dough hook, mix together the flour, ⅓ cup sugar, and 2 teaspoons vanilla.

In a medium saucepan, scald the milk (bring almost to a boil, until milk is just simmering). Allow to sit for 1 minute to cool just slightly.

With mixer on low, add the water-yeast mixture, milk, and melted butter. Add eggs one at a time.

When the dough begins to come together, after 2 to 3 minutes, turn off mixer and scrape down the sides. Raise the speed to high and mix for another 5 to 10 minutes until the dough is shiny, elastic, and smooth. It may seem like a long time to mix, but the result is worth the wait.

Place dough in a greased bowl with a damp towel on top. Allow to rise 1 to 2 hours.

Make the sugar syrup while dough is rising: Combine the water, sugar, and vanilla in a small saucepan. Bring to a low boil until the sugar has dissolved. Set aside and cool. This syrup can be kept in the fridge for 2 to 3 months and makes enough for at least 2 batches of babka (6 medium babkas).

Prepare three 8½-by-4½-inch greased loaf pans. Note: you can also make two larger round babkas that can be baked on baking sheets.

To make filling: Mix the softened cream cheese with drained pineapple and shredded coconut, and stir to combine.

continued

Cut the dough into three equal parts (use a food scale for precision). Roll out one part into a rectangle. Spread with one-third of the filling and roll up along the shorter side (to create more swirls inside). See pages 92–93 for shaping.

Once the dough is formed into a swirled log, cut it straight down the middle so the filling is exposed. Cut ½ inch off each end. Layer each cut piece on top of one another and twist. Place in a greased loaf pan.

Repeat with the other two pieces of babka dough. Lightly drape a kitchen towel over the top of pans. Allow to rise another 30 minutes. Preheat oven to 350°F while the dough rises.

Bake for approximately 35 minutes. The edges should be slightly brown and the middle should be slightly doughy.

Allow to cool for 5 to 10 minutes. Using a butter knife, loosen sides of the babka from the pan and place on wire rack to cool.

After babka has baked and cooled, combine white chocolate chips with vegetable oil in a microwave-safe bowl. Microwave for 30 second intervals, mixing in between with a small spatula, until completely melted and smooth.

Drizzle melted white chocolate on top of each babka and allow to set.

PEANUT BUTTER AND JELLY BABKA

I absolutely love peanut butter and jelly desserts—salty peanut butter combines perfectly with sweet jelly, and when stuffed inside babka (or challah or hamantaschen or rugelach) it's like a sweet peanut butter and jelly sandwich that sends me straight back to my childhood lunches. I prefer using creamy peanut butter and raspberry jam, but use any combination you like.

Yields 3 loaves

INGREDIENTS

FOR THE DOUGH:

1 tablespoon dry active yeast

⅓ cup + ½ teaspoon sugar

½ cup lukewarm water

4½ cups unbleached all-purpose flour

2 teaspoons vanilla

½ cup whole or 2% milk (or almond milk)

¾ cup (1½ sticks) unsalted butter (or margarine), melted

2 eggs

FOR THE SUGAR SYRUP:

⅔ cup water

1 cup sugar

1 teaspoon vanilla

FOR THE FILLING:

1 cup creamy, all-natural peanut butter

¾ cup jelly

INSTRUCTIONS

For the dough: Place the yeast and ½ teaspoon sugar in a small bowl. Add the lukewarm water and stir gently to mix. Set aside until foamy, 5 to 10 minutes.

In a stand mixer fitted with a dough hook, mix together the flour, ⅓ cup sugar, and 2 teaspoons vanilla.

In a medium saucepan, scald the milk (bring almost to a boil, until milk is just simmering). Allow to sit for 1 minute to cool just slightly.

With mixer on low, add the water-yeast mixture, milk, and melted butter. Add eggs one at a time.

When the dough begins to come together, after 2 to 3 minutes, turn off mixer and scrape down the sides. Raise the speed to high and mix for another 5 to 10 minutes until the dough is shiny, elastic, and smooth. It may seem like a long time to mix, but the result is worth the wait.

Place dough in a greased bowl with a damp towel on top. Allow to rise 1 to 2 hours.

Make the sugar syrup while dough is rising: Combine water, sugar, and vanilla in a small saucepan. Bring to a low boil until sugar has dissolved. Set aside and cool. This syrup can be kept in the fridge for 2 to 3 months and makes enough for at least 2 batches of babka (6 medium babkas).

Prepare three 8½-by-4½-inch greased loaf pans. Note: you can also make two larger round babkas that can be baked on baking sheets.

Cut the dough into three equal parts (use a food scale for precision). Roll out one part into a rectangle. Spread with one-third each of the peanut butter, then jelly, and roll up along the shorter side (to create more swirls inside). See pages 92–93 for shaping.

Once the dough is formed into a swirled log, cut it straight down the middle so the filling is exposed. Cut ½ inch off each end. Layer each cut piece on top of one another and twist. Place in a greased loaf pan.

Repeat with the other two pieces of babka dough. Lightly drape a kitchen towel over the top of pans. Allow to rise another 30 minutes. Preheat oven to 350°F while the dough rises.

Bake for 20 minutes. Brush each babka with two layers of sugar syrup. Place back in the oven for approximately 15 minutes. The edges should be slightly brown and the middle should be slightly doughy.

When the babkas come out of the oven, immediately brush each with another 3 light layers of sugar syrup.

Allow to cool for 5 to 10 minutes. Using a butter knife, loosen sides of the babka from the pan and place on wire rack to cool.

ONION JAM BABKA

When onions are cooked low and slow you get sweet, caramelized onions that are perfect for topping burgers, sandwiches, or stuffing inside babka. Onion jam makes a fantastic condiment for all kinds of baked goods. I would serve this as an appetizer as opposed to a dessert.

Yields 3 loaves

INGREDIENTS

FOR THE DOUGH:

1 tablespoon dry active yeast

3 tablespoons + ½ teaspoon sugar

½ cup lukewarm water

4½ cups unbleached all-purpose flour

¼ teaspoon salt

½ cup whole or 2% milk (or almond milk)

¾ cup (1½ sticks) unsalted butter (or margarine), melted

2 eggs

FOR THE FILLING:

1 cup Savory Onion Jam (page 23)

FOR THE TOPPING:

3 ounces goat cheese, crumbled (optional)

INSTRUCTIONS

Place the yeast and ½ teaspoon sugar in a small bowl. Add the lukewarm water and stir gently to mix. Set aside until foamy, 5 to 10 minutes.

In a stand mixer fitted with a dough hook, mix together the flour, 3 tablespoons sugar, and salt.

In a medium saucepan, scald the milk (bring almost to a boil, until milk is just simmering). Allow to sit for 1 minute to cool just slightly.

With mixer on low, add the water-yeast mixture, milk, and melted butter. Add eggs one at a time.

When the dough begins to come together, after 2 to 3 minutes, turn off mixer and scrape down the sides. Raise the speed to high and mix for another 5 to 10 minutes until the dough is shiny and elastic. It may seem like a long time to mix, but the result is worth the wait. The dough should be very shiny, elastic, and smooth.

Place dough in a greased bowl with a damp towel on top. Allow to rise 1 to 2 hours.

Prepare three 8½-by-4½-inch greased loaf pans. Note: you can also make two larger round babkas that can be baked on baking sheets.

Cut the dough into three equal parts (use a food scale for precision). Roll out one part into a rectangle. Spread with ⅓ cup of the Savory Onion Jam and roll up along the shorter side (to create more swirls inside). See pages 92–93 for shaping.

Once the dough is formed into a swirled log, cut it straight down the middle so the filling is exposed. Cut ½ inch off each end. Layer each cut piece on top of one another and twist. Place in a greased loaf pan.

Repeat with the other two pieces of babka dough. Lightly drape a kitchen towel over the top of pans. Allow to rise another 30 minutes. Preheat oven to 350°F while the dough rises.

Top each babka with one-third of the cheese, if using.

Bake for approximately 35 minutes. The edges should be slightly brown and the middle should be slightly doughy.

Allow to cool for 5 to 10 minutes. Using a butter knife, loosen sides of the babka from the pan and place on wire rack to cool.

GUAVA AND CHEESE BABKA

This recipe was inspired by my friend and colleague Jennifer Stempel, who loves combining her Cuban and Jewish heritage in dishes like Cuban matzo ball soup, plantain knishes, and guava hamantaschen. Guava and cream cheese pastries are one of the most classic sweets at Porto's, a famous bakery in Los Angeles that we both adore, and this babka is inspired by those beloved treats.

Yields 3 loaves

INGREDIENTS

FOR THE DOUGH:

1 tablespoon dry active yeast

⅓ cup + ½ teaspoon sugar

½ cup lukewarm water

4½ cups unbleached all-purpose flour

¼ teaspoon salt

2 teaspoons vanilla

1 teaspoon fresh orange zest

½ cup whole or 2% milk (or almond milk)

¾ cup (1½ sticks) unsalted butter (or margarine), melted

2 eggs

FOR THE SUGAR SYRUP:

⅔ cup water

1 cup sugar

1 teaspoon vanilla

FOR THE FILLING:

12 ounces cream cheese, softened

6 ounces guava paste

INSTRUCTIONS

For the dough: Place the yeast and ½ teaspoon sugar in a small bowl. Add the lukewarm water and stir gently to mix. Set aside until foamy, 5 to 10 minutes.

In a stand mixer fitted with a dough hook, mix together the flour, ⅓ cup sugar, salt, 2 teaspoons vanilla, and orange zest.

In a medium saucepan, scald the milk (bring almost to a boil, until milk is just simmering). Allow to sit for 1 minute to cool just slightly.

With mixer on low, add the water-yeast mixture, milk, and melted butter. Add eggs one at a time.

When the dough begins to come together, after 2 to 3 minutes, turn off mixer and scrape down the sides. Raise the speed to high and mix for another 5 to 10 minutes until the dough is shiny, elastic, and smooth. It may seem like a long time to mix, but the result is worth the wait.

Place the dough in a greased bowl with a damp towel on top. Allow to rise 1 to 2 hours.

Make the sugar syrup while dough is rising: Combine the water, sugar, and vanilla in a small saucepan. Bring to a low boil until the sugar has dissolved. Set aside and cool. This syrup can be kept in the fridge for 2 to 3 months and makes enough syrup for at least 2 batches of babka (6 medium babkas).

Prepare three 8½-by-4½-inch greased loaf pans. Note: you can also make two larger round babkas that can be baked on baking sheets.

Cut the dough into three equal parts (use a food scale for precision). Roll out one part into a rectangle. Spread with one-third each of the cream cheese, then guava paste, and roll up along the shorter side (to create more swirls inside). See pages 92–93 for shaping.

Once the dough is formed into a swirled log, cut it straight down the middle so the filling is exposed. Cut ½ inch off each end. Layer each cut piece on top of one another and twist. Place in a greased loaf pan.

Repeat with the other two pieces of babka dough. Lightly drape a kitchen towel over the top of pans. Allow to rise another 30 minutes. Preheat oven to 350°F while the dough rises.

Bake for 20 minutes. Brush each babka with two layers of sugar syrup. Place back in the oven for approximately 15 minutes. The edges should be slightly brown and the middle should be slightly doughy.

When the babkas come out of the oven, immediately brush each with another 3 light layers of sugar syrup.

Allow to cool for 5 to 10 minutes. Using a butter knife, loosen sides of the babka from the pan and place on wire rack to cool.

BUFFALO BLUE CHEESE BABKA

I realize this combination of babka, hot sauce, and blue cheese may sound a bit bizarre, but the combination is spicy, addictive, and delicious. Serve this up for friends who love the taste of chicken wings or who just love the combination of spicy and cheesy flavors.

Yields 3 loaves

INGREDIENTS

FOR THE DOUGH:

1 tablespoon dry active yeast

3 tablespoons + ½ teaspoon sugar

½ cup lukewarm water

4½ cups unbleached all-purpose flour

¼ teaspoon salt

½ cup whole or 2% milk (or almond milk)

¾ cup (1½ sticks) unsalted butter (or margarine), melted

2 eggs

FOR THE FILLING:

½ cup (1 stick) unsalted butter, softened

¼ cup hot sauce

Pinch salt

Pinch pepper

¼–⅓ cup blue cheese

INSTRUCTIONS

To make the dough: Place the yeast and ½ teaspoon sugar in a small bowl. Add the lukewarm water and stir gently to mix. Set aside until foamy, 5 to 10 minutes.

In a stand mixer fitted with a dough hook, mix together the flour, 3 tablespoons sugar, and salt.

In a medium saucepan, scald the milk (bring almost to a boil, until milk is just simmering). Allow to sit for 1 minute to cool just slightly.

With mixer on low, add the water-yeast mixture, milk, and melted butter. Add eggs one at a time.

When the dough begins to come together, after 2 to 3 minutes, turn off mixer and scrape down the sides. Raise the speed to high and mix for another 5 to 10 minutes until the dough is shiny, elastic, and smooth. It may seem like a long time to mix, but the result is worth the wait.

Place the dough in a greased bowl with a damp towel on top. Allow to rise 1 to 2 hours.

Prepare three 8½-by-4½-inch greased loaf pans. Note: you can also make two larger round babkas that can be baked on baking sheets.

To make the filling: Combine the softened butter with hot sauce and a pinch salt and pepper.

continued

Cut the dough into three equal parts (use a food scale for precision). Roll out one part into a rectangle. Spread with one-third of the hot sauce and butter mixture, then sprinkle with one-third of the blue cheese and roll up along the shorter side (to create more swirls inside). See pages 92–93 for shaping.

Once the dough is formed into a swirled log, cut it straight down the middle so the filling is exposed. Cut ½ inch off each end. Layer each cut piece on top of one another and twist. Place in a greased loaf pan.

Repeat with other two pieces of babka dough. Lightly drape a kitchen towel over the top of pans. Allow to rise another 30 minutes. Preheat oven to 350°F while the dough rises.

Bake for approximately 35 minutes. The edges should be slightly brown and the middle should be slightly doughy.

Allow to cool for 5 to 10 minutes. Using a butter knife, loosen sides of the babka from the pan and place on top of parchment wire rack to cool.

LEFTOVER REMIX:
SAVORY BABKA CROUTONS

There's nothing worse than homemade bread or cakes going to waste. And there's nothing better on top of a salad or creamy bowl of soup than some homemade croutons—especially savory babka croutons. If you can't make your leftovers into croutons right away, place remaining babka in a Ziploc bag in the freezer until ready to make.

Yields about 1½ cups croutons

INGREDIENTS

2 slices leftover savory babka, cut into cubes

1–2 tablespoons olive oil

Pinch salt and pepper

INSTRUCTIONS

If babka is still soft, spread babka cubes out on a baking sheet and leave out at room temperature for a few hours to get more stale.

Preheat oven to 375°F.

Drizzle olive oil, then sprinkle salt and pepper over babka cubes. Use hands to coat babka cubes in seasoning and oil. (You can also use dried herbs such as basil, herbes de Provence, or za'atar to season during this step.)

Bake for 12 to 15 minutes, turning at least once, until babka is crisp and golden.

OLIVE TAPENADE BABKA

Tapenade is one of the ingredients I most enjoy baking inside savory treats. Tapenade is easy to make but also readily available at most stores. The saltiness of the olives plays nicely off the slight sweetness of the babka dough.

Yields 3 loaves

INGREDIENTS

FOR THE DOUGH:

1 tablespoon dry active yeast

3 tablespoons + ½ teaspoon sugar

½ cup lukewarm water

4½ cups unbleached all-purpose flour

¼ teaspoon salt

½ cup whole or 2% milk (or almond milk)

¾ cup (1½ sticks) unsalted butter (or margarine), melted

2 eggs

FOR THE FILLING:

1 cup Mixed Olive Tapenade (page 22)

FOR THE TOPPING:

3 ounces goat cheese, crumbled (optional)

INSTRUCTIONS

Place the yeast and ½ teaspoon sugar in a small bowl. Add the lukewarm water and stir gently to mix. Set aside until foamy, 5 to 10 minutes.

In a stand mixer fitted with a dough hook, mix together flour, 3 tablespoons sugar, and salt.

In a medium saucepan, scald the milk (bring almost to a boil, until milk is just simmering). Allow to sit for 1 minute to cool just slightly.

With mixer on low, add water-yeast mixture, milk, and melted butter. Add eggs one at a time.

When the dough begins to come together, after 2 to 3 minutes, turn off mixer and scrape down the sides. Raise the speed to high and mix for another 5 to 10 minutes until the dough is shiny, elastic, and smooth. It may seem like a long time to mix, but the result is worth the wait.

Place the dough in a greased bowl with a damp towel on top. Allow to rise 1 to 2 hours.

Prepare three 8½-by-4½-inch greased loaf pans. Note: you can also make two larger round babkas that can be baked on baking sheets.

Cut the dough into three equal parts (use a food scale for precision). Roll out one part into a rectangle. Spread with ⅓ cup of the Mixed Olive Tapenade on each and roll up along the shorter side (to create more swirls inside). See pages 92–93 for shaping.

Once the dough is formed into a swirled log, cut it straight down the middle so the filling is exposed. Cut ½ inch off each end. Layer each cup piece on top of one another and twist. Place in a greased loaf pan.

continued

Repeat with other two pieces of babka dough. Lightly drape a kitchen towel over the top of pans. Allow to rise another 30 minutes. Preheat oven to 350°F while the dough rises.

Top each babka with one-third of the cheese, if using.

Bake for approximately 35 minutes. The edges should be slightly brown and the middle should be slightly doughy.

Allow to cool for 5 to 10 minutes. Using a butter knife, loosen sides of the babka from the pan and place on top of parchment wire rack to cool.

FIG JAM AND GOAT CHEESE BABKA

This babka isn't quite sweet, and it isn't quite savory, but it is quite fancy and would go great with a nice bottle of chilled white wine. Fig jam is easy to find in the cheese section of a good market. Combine the fig jam with tangy goat cheese and you've got a cheese plate–lover's dream babka.

Yields 3 loaves

INGREDIENTS

FOR THE DOUGH:

1 tablespoon dry active yeast

3 tablespoons + ½ teaspoon sugar

½ cup lukewarm water

4½ cups unbleached all-purpose flour

¼ teaspoon salt

½ cup whole or 2% milk (or almond milk)

¾ cup (1½ sticks) unsalted butter (or margarine), melted

2 teaspoons herbes de Provence

2 eggs

FOR THE FILLING:

¾ cup fig jam

3 ounces goat cheese

INSTRUCTIONS

Place the yeast and ½ teaspoon sugar in a small bowl. Add the lukewarm water and stir gently to mix. Set aside until foamy, 5 to 10 minutes.

In a stand mixer fitted with a dough hook, mix together the flour, 3 tablespoons sugar, and salt.

In a medium saucepan, scald the milk (bring almost to a boil, until milk is just simmering). Allow to sit for 1 minute to cool just slightly.

With mixer on low, add the water-yeast mixture, milk, melted butter, and herbes de Provence. Add eggs one at a time.

When the dough begins to come together, after 2 to 3 minutes, turn off mixer and scrape down the sides. Raise the speed to high and mix for another 5 to 10 minutes until the dough is shiny, elastic, and smooth. It may seem like a long time to mix, but the result is worth the wait.

Place dough in a greased bowl with a damp towel on top. Allow to rise 1 to 2 hours.

Prepare three 8½-by-4½-inch greased loaf pans. Note: you can also make two larger round babkas that can be baked on baking sheets.

continued

Cut the dough into three equal parts (use a food scale for precision). Roll out one part into a rectangle. Spread with ¼ cup of the fig jam on each rolled out babka dough. Top with an even layer of crumbled goat cheese, approximately 1 ounce on each babka, and roll up along the shorter side (to create more swirls inside). See pages 92–93 for shaping.

Once the dough is formed into a swirled log, cut it straight down the middle so the filling is exposed. Cut ½ inch off each end. Layer each cut piece on top of one another and twist. Place in a greased loaf pan.

Repeat with other two pieces of babka dough. Lightly drape a kitchen towel over the top of pans. Allow to rise another 30 minutes. Preheat oven to 350°F while the dough rises.

Bake for approximately 35 minutes. The edges should be slightly brown and the middle should be slightly doughy.

Allow to cool for 5 to 10 minutes. Using a butter knife, loosen sides of the babka from the pan and place on top of parchment wire rack to cool.

BIRTHDAY CAKE BABKA

This whimsical babka recipe is a cross between funfetti birthday cake, coffee cake, and a traditional sweet babka. It is decadent, delicious, and my daughter's favorite.

Yields 3 loaves

INGREDIENTS

FOR THE DOUGH:

1 tablespoon dry active yeast

⅓ cup + ½ teaspoon sugar

½ cup lukewarm water

4½ cups unbleached all-purpose flour

2 teaspoons vanilla

½ cup whole or 2% milk (or almond milk)

¾ cup (1½ sticks) unsalted butter (or margarine), melted

2 eggs

FOR THE FILLING:

12 ounces cream cheese, softened

¾ cup confectioners' sugar

1 teaspoon vanilla

⅛ teaspoon baking powder

Pinch salt

¼ cup colored sprinkles

Note: It is best to use jimmies or oblong sprinkles, not round (nonpareil) sprinkles.

INSTRUCTIONS

To make the dough: Place the yeast and ½ teaspoon sugar in a small bowl. Add the lukewarm water and stir gently to mix. Set aside until foamy, 5 to 10 minutes.

In a stand mixer fitted with a dough hook, mix together the flour, ⅓ cup sugar, and 2 teaspoons vanilla.

In a medium saucepan, scald the milk (bring almost to a boil, until milk is just simmering). Allow to sit for 1 minute to cool just slightly.

With mixer on low, add the water-yeast mixture, milk, and melted butter. Add eggs one at a time.

When the dough begins to come together, after 2 to 3 minutes, turn off mixer and scrape down the sides. Raise the speed to high and mix for another 5 to 10 minutes until the dough is shiny and elastic.

Place dough in a greased bowl with a damp towel on top. Allow to rise until it has doubled, about 1 to 2 hours.

While dough is rising, make the filling and the topping.

To make the filling: Beat the softened cream cheese, powdered sugar, 1 teaspoon vanilla, baking powder, and salt. Fold in the sprinkles.

continued

FOR THE CRUMB TOPPING:

¼ cup sugar

⅓ cup packed brown sugar

½ cup (1 stick) unsalted butter, melted

1⅓ cups unbleached all-purpose flour

2 tablespoons colored sprinkles

FOR THE FROSTING:

3 cups confectioners' sugar

5–6 tablespoons milk

Pinch salt

To make the crumb topping: Combine the sugars in a small bowl. Stir in the melted butter and the flour. Add the sprinkles and combine using fingers.

Prepare three 8½-by-4½-inch greased loaf pans. Note: you can also make two larger round babkas that can be baked on baking sheets.

Cut the dough into three equal parts (use a food scale for precision). Roll out one part into a rectangle. Spread with one-third of the cream cheese filling and roll up along the shorter side (to create more swirls inside). See pages 92–93 for shaping.

Once the dough is formed into a swirled log, cut it straight down the middle so the filling is exposed. Cut ½ inch off each end. Layer each cut piece on top of one another and twist. Place in a greased loaf pan.

Repeat with other two pieces of babka dough. Lightly drape a kitchen towel over the top of pans. Allow to rise another 30 minutes. Preheat oven to 350°F while the dough rises.

Before baking, add one-third of the crumb topping on each babka. Bake for 30 to 35 minutes. The edges should be slightly brown and the middle should be slightly doughy.

Allow to cool for 5 to 10 minutes. Using a butter knife, loosen sides of the babkas from the pans and place on top of parchment wire rack to cool.

Place babkas on a platter.

To make the frosting: Combine confectioners' sugar, milk, and salt in a bowl. Drizzle on top of each babka.

Short cut: If you don't want to make the crumb topping and frosting, you can skip those steps. After the babka has baked and cooled, combine 1 cup (approximately 6 ounces) white chocolate chips with 1 tablespoon vegetable oil in a microwave-safe bowl. Microwave for 30-second intervals, mixing in between with a small spatula, until completely melted and smooth. Drizzle melted white chocolate on top of each babka and allow to set.

DOUBLE CHOCOLATE COOKIE BABKA

I am an absolute nut about Oreo cookies, and this double chocolate Oreo babka is seriously decadent. With two kinds of chocolate in the dough plus a sweet, cream cheese filling and crushed Oreo cookies, don't expect any leftovers.

Yields 3 loaves

INGREDIENTS

FOR THE DOUGH:

1 tablespoon yeast

⅓ cup + ½ teaspoon sugar

½ cup lukewarm water

4½ cups + 2 tablespoons flour, + additional 1–2 tablespoons, if needed

¼ cup cocoa powder (I prefer Hershey's Special Dark Cocoa powder)

½ teaspoon cinnamon

2 teaspoons vanilla

½ cup whole or 2% milk (or almond milk)

¾ cup (1½ sticks) unsalted butter (or margarine), melted

2 eggs

¼ cup (1½ ounces) milk chocolate chips, melted

INSTRUCTIONS

To make the dough: Place the yeast and ½ teaspoon sugar in a small bowl. Add the lukewarm water and stir gently to mix. Set aside until foamy, 5 to 10 minutes.

In a stand mixer fitted with a dough hook, mix together 4½ cups of the flour, cocoa powder, cinnamon, ⅓ cup sugar, and 2 teaspoons vanilla.

In a medium saucepan, scald the milk (bring almost to a boil, until milk is just simmering). Allow to sit for 1 minute to cool just slightly.

Put mixer on low and add the water-yeast mixture, then the butter and milk. Add the eggs one at a time. Add the melted chocolate. If the dough seems too wet, add 1 to 2 additional tablespoons of flour until dough doesn't stick to sides of bowl.

When the dough begins to come together, after about 3 to 5 minutes, raise the speed to high and mix for another 5 to 10 minutes until the dough is shiny and elastic.

Place dough in a greased bowl with a damp towel on top. Allow to rise about 1 to 2 hours.

continued

FOR THE FILLING:

16 ounces cream cheese, at room temperature

½ cup + 2 tablespoons powdered sugar

1 teaspoon vanilla

Pinch salt

1–1½ cups crushed Oreo cookies

FOR THE SYRUP:

⅔ cup water

1 cup sugar

1 teaspoon vanilla

While dough is rising, make the filling: Beat the cream cheese with the powdered sugar, vanilla, and salt until smooth. Set aside.

Prepare three 8½-by-4½-inch greased loaf pans. Note: you can also make two larger round babkas that can be baked on baking sheets.

Cut the dough into three equal parts (use a food scale for precision). Roll out one part into a rectangle. Spread with one-third of the cream cheese filling, sprinkle with one-third of the crushed Oreo cookies, and roll up along the shorter side (to create more swirls inside). See pages 92–93 for shaping.

Once the dough is formed into a swirled log, cut it straight down the middle so the filling is exposed. Cut ½ inch off each end. Layer each cut piece on top of one another and twist. Place in a greased loaf pan.

Repeat with the other two pieces of babka dough. Lightly drape a kitchen towel over the top of pans. Allow to rise another 30 minutes. Preheat oven to 350°F while the dough rises.

While the babka is baking, make the syrup: Combine the water, sugar, and vanilla in a small saucepan. Bring to a boil on medium-high heat. Once it comes to a boil, remove from heat and swirl around to ensure all the sugar is dissolved.

About 25 minutes into baking, spoon about ¼ cup of the syrup onto each babka.

Put back into the oven for another 10 minutes. The edges should be slightly brown and the middle should be slightly doughy.

When you take the babkas out of the oven after they have baked completely, immediately brush an additional ¼ cup sugar syrup onto the top of all three babkas. It may seem like a lot of syrup, but this ensures a moist and gooey babka.

Allow to cool for 5 to 10 minutes. Using a butter knife, loosen sides of the babkas from the pans and place on wire baking rack to cool.

DOUBLE LAYER CARAMEL AND CHOCOLATE BABKA

Of all the babkas I have baked and created and tested, I think this is the most beautiful, the most impressive, and the most scrumptious. By layering two pieces of babka dough on top of one another with fillings, you double the luscious swirls inside.

Yields 1 large babka

INGREDIENTS

FOR THE DOUGH:

1 tablespoon dry active yeast

⅓ cup + ½ teaspoon sugar

½ cup lukewarm water

4½ cups unbleached all-purpose flour

2 teaspoons vanilla

½ cup whole or 2% milk (or almond milk)

¾ cup (1½ sticks) unsalted butter (or margarine), melted

2 eggs

FOR THE SUGAR SYRUP:

⅔ cup water

1 cup sugar

1 teaspoon vanilla

FOR THE CHOCOLATE FILLING:

1 batch Chocolate Filling (page 26)

INSTRUCTIONS

To make the dough: Place the yeast and ½ teaspoon sugar in a small bowl. Add the lukewarm water and stir gently to mix. Set aside until foamy, around 5 to 10 minutes.

In a stand mixer fitted with a dough hook, mix together the flour, ⅓ cup sugar, and 2 teaspoons vanilla.

In a medium saucepan, scald the milk (bring almost to a boil, until milk is just simmering). Allow to sit for 1 minute to cool just slightly.

With mixer on low, add the water-yeast mixture, milk, and melted butter. Add eggs one at a time.

When the dough begins to come together, after 2 to 3 minutes, turn off mixer and scrape down the sides. Raise the speed to high and mix for another 5 to 10 minutes until the dough is shiny, elastic, and smooth. It may seem like a long time to mix, but the result is worth the wait.

Place the dough in a greased bowl with a damp towel on top. Allow to rise 1 to 2 hours.

Make the sugar syrup while dough is rising: Combine the water, sugar, and vanilla in a small saucepan. Bring to a low boil until sugar has dissolved. Set aside and cool. This syrup can be kept in the fridge for 2 to 3 months and makes enough for at least 2 batches of babka (6 medium babkas).

continued

FOR THE CARAMEL FILLING:

20 soft caramel candies, unwrapped

2 tablespoons unsalted butter

½ cup mini chocolate chips

To make caramel filling: Add caramels and butter in a glass bowl. Microwave for 30-second intervals, mixing in between with a small spatula, until completely melted and smooth. Set aside.

Prepare a large 9- or 10-inch greased loaf pan.

Divide the dough into two equal parts (use a food scale for precision). Roll out one each section of dough into a rectangle on lightly floured work surface.

Spread one piece of the dough with the Chocolate Filling. Spread the other piece of dough with the melted caramel filling. Top caramel with mini chocolate chips, lightly pressing chips into caramel.

Lay the pieces of dough on top of one another and roll up along the shorter side (to create more swirls inside). See pages 92–93 for shaping.

Once the dough is formed into a swirled log, cut it straight down the middle so the filling is exposed. Cut ½ inch off each end. Layer each cut piece on top of one another and twist. Place in the greased loaf pan. Allow to rise another 20 to 30 minutes. Preheat oven to 350°F while the dough rises.

About 25 minutes into baking, spoon about ¼ cup of the syrup onto the babka. Put back into the oven for another 10 minutes. The edges should be slightly brown and the middle should be slightly doughy.

When you take the babka out of the oven after it has baked completely, immediately brush an additional ¼ cup sugar syrup on top of the babka.

Allow to cool for 5 to 10 minutes. Using a butter knife, loosen sides of the babkas from the pans and place on wire baking rack to cool.

LEFTOVER REMIX:
BABKA FRENCH TOAST

We know that challah French toast is a big crowd-pleaser. But babka French toast makes brunch a little more decadent. You can also try making a savory babka French toast topped with fried eggs—just leave out the sugar, vanilla, and cinnamon from this recipe. Use one of your savory babka loaves, and you'll have a truly unique breakfast.

Yields 2 to 4 servings

INGREDIENTS

2 large eggs

½ cup milk

1 tablespoon sugar

½ teaspoon vanilla

¼ teaspoon cinnamon (optional)

Pinch salt

4–6 slices leftover babka

Butter, for cooking

INSTRUCTIONS

Whisk together eggs, milk, sugar, vanilla, cinnamon, and salt and place in a large shallow dish.

Soak pieces of babka in the egg-milk mixture and allow them to sit for 1 to 2 minutes until liquid has been absorbed on each side. You may need to turn each piece. Repeat with remaining pieces of babka.

Heat 1 tablespoon of butter in a large skillet over medium heat. Cook babka in batches, until golden brown on each side. Serve with powdered sugar and maple syrup.

BAGELS

Before writing this book, I had never given so much thought to the history and process of bagels. I am a Jewish New Yorker, and so for me crusty, chewy bagels were simply part of the landscape.

It is well known that bagels were brought to New York City by the Jewish immigrants of Eastern Europe, more specifically Poland, like my relatives. What may be lesser known about the history of bagels is that according to Maria Balinska in her book *The Bagel: The Surprising History of a Modest Bread,* the Jews of Poland favored bagels because their crusty outsides enabled them to last longer; the bagels went stale slower than regular bread because they were boiled first.

Making bagels at home is certainly the most complicated task you'll perform using this book, but it is so rewarding. Creating a bagel with a crispy, crusty outside (akin to those New York–style bagels so many of us covet), a chewy inside, and a smooth shape is more about the process and method than it is about the recipe itself. Most bagel recipes are fairly similar in terms of ingredients, but the process for making them can vary drastically.

HOW THE DOUGH SHOULD FEEL

Unlike challah or babka, bagel dough should feel quite firm. The tougher dough will produce a good crust and chew. You should be able to roll it into a rope to shape, but it will be more difficult to work with than challah. The dough should be quite smooth.

RISING

I suggest letting the formed bagels rise in the fridge for 12 to 18 hours before baking. This allows a slow fermentation.

STORAGE

If you aren't planning to consume all the bagels the same day they are baked, you can store them in an airtight container or bag. But the better method is to allow them to cool completely and then place them in a freezer bag and freeze until ready to use.

FLOUR

You must use a high-gluten flour such as King Arthur unbleached bread flour.

ESSENTIAL TOOLS

Pizza stone for baking

Metal spider for removing bagels from their water bath

Baking sheets

Silicone baking mats

SPECIAL NOTES

The bagel dough should be mixed slowly at a low speed for around 5 to 7 minutes. At first it may not seem like the dough is coming together, but just be patient and give it time. Walk out of the room if you must.

Malt barley is an essential ingredient for both the dough and the water bath. It can be found on Amazon, in Whole Foods markets, or in the baking aisle of other major supermarkets. You can make the bagels without it, but if you want that true, authentic New York-style bagel, I recommend putting in the time to procure the malt barley.

Invest in a good pizza stone if you don't already have one. I bought mine nearly ten years ago for $50 from Williams-Sonoma. I am still using that same stone.

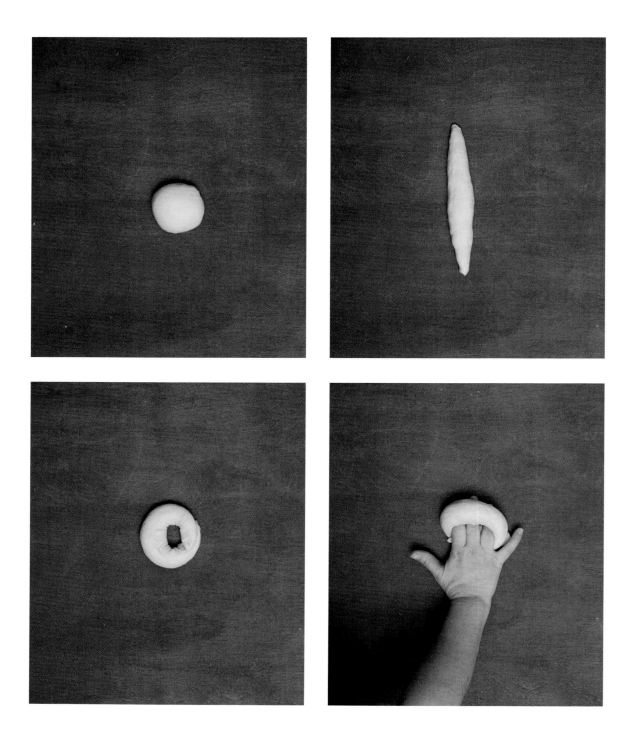

BASIC BAGELS

Admittedly, this recipe is the most complicated one you'll encounter in the book. Keep in mind that making a good bagel is less about the ingredients and more about the process. So take your time when making bagels, and don't be upset if your first batch is misshapen or is not quite perfect. This is a recipe to practice over time. When you get it right, you will feel like you hit the jackpot. You really can make great, New York–style bagels at home without even importing any New York City water.

Yields 8 to 10 bagels

INGREDIENTS

2 teaspoons dry yeast

½ teaspoon sugar

1½ cups lukewarm water

4 cups unbleached bread flour

2 teaspoons + pinch salt

1 heaping tablespoon + 2 teaspoons malt barley

INSTRUCTIONS

Place the yeast and sugar in a small bowl or liquid measuring cup. Add the lukewarm water and stir gently to mix. Let stand 5 to 10 minutes.

Meanwhile, add flour, 2 teaspoons salt, and 1 heaping tablespoon malt barley in a stand mixer fitted with a hook attachment.

Once the yeast-water mixture has started bubbling on top, add to mixer bowl and start mixing on low speed. When the dough begins to come together, 3 to 4 minutes, raise speed to medium-low.

Keep mixing for another 5 to 7 minutes, until dough is elastic, shiny, and dense. Remove from bowl and allow to rest 1 minute.

Divide the dough into 8 to 10 small sections. Each section should measure 3 to 4 ounces (use a food scale for precision), depending on how large you want your bagels.

Roll each section into a ball and place on a baking sheet lined with parchment paper or silicone baking mat. Cover for 10 to 15 minutes.

Shape your bagels: Roll each piece of dough into a 3- to 4-inch rope, tapering ends just slightly. See pages 144–145 for shaping.

One at a time, take the ends of the rope and overlap them just slightly, pinch and then roll with the palm of your hands. If your shape isn't quite uniform, roll the other side of the bagel by placing your palm inside the middle and roll gently until desired shape.

Place rolled bagels back on the baking sheet lined with parchment paper or a silicone baking mat and cover with plastic wrap. Place in the fridge 12 to 18 hours.

When ready to boil and bake, place a pizza stone on the top rack of your oven. Preheat the oven to 500°F. Allow pizza stone to sit in heated oven for 30 minutes.

Bring a wide pot of water to a low boil over medium-high heat. Add 2 teaspoons malt barley and a pinch of salt to the pot.

Do not start boiling your bagels until your oven has completely preheated, because once the bagels boil for 1 to 2 minutes, you want to get the bagels into the oven immediately. Also do not take the bagels out of the fridge too soon, or they may spread and lose their shape.

Once the water is boiling, reduce heat just slightly so it's a robust simmer. Add the puffed side of the bagel into the water first (flatter side should be up). After 30 to 60 seconds, flip the bagel using a spider and let sit another 30 to 60 seconds.

Using your spider once again, remove bagel from water, allow excess water to drip back into the pot, and place the bagel flatter side down into the oven directly onto the heated pizza stone. If you are going to add toppings, add them quickly as you put the bagel into the oven.

After 10 minutes, flip the bagels onto the other side.

Bake another 3 to 5 minutes, depending on how crispy you want the outside of your bagel. Allow to cool and serve immediately.

WHOLE-WHEAT BAGELS

For the times when you want to feel a little healthier about your Sunday bagels and schmear, try a whole-wheat variety. This recipe uses part white flour and part whole-wheat flour, but the result is a bagel that is just as crusty and chewy as its plain counterpart.

Yields 8 to 10 bagels

INGREDIENTS

2 teaspoons dry yeast

½ teaspoon sugar

1½ cups lukewarm water

1½ cups whole-wheat flour

2½ cups unbleached bread flour

2 teaspoons + pinch salt

1 heaping tablespoon + 2 teaspoons malt barley

INSTRUCTIONS

Place the yeast and sugar in a small bowl or liquid measuring cup. Add the lukewarm water and stir gently to mix. Let stand 5 minutes.

Meanwhile, add the flours, 2 teaspoons salt, and 1 heaping tablespoon malt barley in a stand mixer fitted with a hook attachment.

Once the yeast-water mixture has started bubbling on top, add to mixer bowl and start mixing on low speed. When the dough begins to come together, 3 to 4 minutes, raise speed to medium-low.

Keep mixing for another 5 to 7 minutes, until dough is elastic, shiny, and dense. Remove from bowl and allow to rest 1 minute.

Divide dough into 8 to 10 small sections. Each section should measure 3 to 4 ounces (use a food scale for precision), depending on how large you want your bagels.

Roll each section into a ball and place on a baking sheet lined with parchment paper or silicone baking mat. Cover for 10 to 15 minutes.

Shape your bagels: Roll each piece of dough into a 3- to 4-inch rope, tapering ends just slightly. See pages 144–145 for shaping.

One at a time, take the ends of the rope and overlap them just slightly, pinch and then roll with the palm of your hands. If your shape isn't quite uniform, roll the other side of the bagel by placing your palm inside the middle and roll gently until desired shape.

Place rolled bagels back on the baking sheet lined with parchment paper or silicone baking mat and cover with plastic wrap. Place in the fridge 12 to 18 hours.

When ready to boil and bake, place a pizza stone on the top rack of your oven. Preheat the oven to 500°F. Allow pizza stone to sit in heated oven for 30 minutes.

Bring a wide pot of water to a low boil over medium-high heat. Add 2 teaspoons malt barley and a pinch of salt to the pot.

Do not start boiling your bagels until your oven has completely preheated, because once the bagels boil for 1 to 2 minutes, you want to get the bagels into the oven immediately. Also do not take the bagels out of the fridge too soon, or they may spread and lose their shape.

Once the water is boiling, reduce heat just slightly so it's a robust simmer. Add the puffed side of the bagel into the water first (flatter side should be up). After 30 to 60 seconds, flip the bagel using a spider and let sit another 30 to 60 seconds.

Using your spider once again, remove bagel from water, allow excess water to drip back into the pot, and place the bagel flatter side down into the oven directly onto the heated pizza stone. If you are going to add toppings, add them quickly as you put the bagel into the oven.

After 10 minutes, flip the bagels onto the other side.

Bake another 3 to 5 minutes depending on how crispy you want the outside of your bagel. Allow to cool and serve immediately.

RYE BAGELS

Both caraway and rye flour can be acquired tastes for some people, but I find the smell and taste of caraway to be intoxicating. And while you could serve a rye bagel with cream cheese and tomato, I would pile it high with pastrami, turkey, and some coleslaw.

Yields 8 to 10 bagels

INGREDIENTS

2 teaspoons dry yeast

½ teaspoon sugar

1½ cups lukewarm water

1 cup rye flour

3 cups unbleached bread flour

2 teaspoons + pinch salt

1 heaping tablespoon + 2 teaspoons malt barley

2 tablespoons caraway seeds, + additional, for topping

Coarse sea salt (optional)

INSTRUCTIONS

Place the yeast and sugar in a small bowl or liquid measuring cup. Add the lukewarm water and stir gently to mix. Let stand 5 minutes.

Meanwhile, add the flours, 2 teaspoons salt, and 1 heaping tablespoon malt barley in a stand mixer fitted with a hook attachment.

Once the yeast-water mixture has started bubbling on top, add to mixer bowl and start mixing on low speed. Add the caraway seeds and continue mixing. When the dough begins to come together, 3 to 4 minutes, raise speed to medium-low.

Keep mixing for another 5 to 7 minutes, until dough is elastic, shiny, and dense. Remove from bowl and allow to rest 1 minute.

Divide into 8 to 10 small sections. Each section should measure 3 to 4 ounces (use a food scale for precision), depending on how large you want your bagels.

Roll each section into a ball and place on a baking sheet lined with parchment paper or silicone baking mat. Cover for 10 to 15 minutes.

Shape your bagels: Roll each piece of dough into a 3- to 4-inch rope, tapering ends just slightly. See pages 144–145 for shaping.

One at a time, take the ends of the rope and overlap them just slightly, pinch and then roll with the palm of your hands. If your shape isn't quite uniform, roll the other side of the bagel by placing your palm inside the middle and roll gently until desired shape.

Place rolled bagels back on the baking sheet lined with parchment paper or silicone baking mat and cover with plastic wrap. Place in the fridge 12 to 18 hours.

When ready to boil and bake, place a pizza stone on the top rack of your oven. Preheat the oven to 500°F. Allow pizza stone to sit in heated oven for 30 minutes.

Bring a wide pot of water to a low boil over medium-high heat. Add 2 teaspoons malt barley and a pinch of salt to the pot.

Do not start boiling your bagels until your oven has completely preheated, because once the bagels boil for 1 to 2 minutes, you want to get the bagels into the oven immediately. Also do not take the bagels out of the fridge too soon, or they may spread and lose their shape.

Once the water is boiling, reduce heat just slightly so it's a robust simmer. Add the puffed side of the bagel into the water first (flatter side should be up). After 30 to 60 seconds, flip the bagel using a spider and let sit another 30 to 60 seconds.

Using your spider once again, remove bagel from water, allow excess water to drip back into the pot, and place the bagel flatter side down into the oven directly onto the heated pizza stone. Quickly sprinkle the bagels with additional caraway seeds and coarse sea salt, if desired, and put the bagels into the oven.

After 10 minutes, flip the bagels onto the other side.

Bake another 3 to 5 minutes depending on how crispy you want the outside of your bagel. Allow to cool and serve immediately.

JALAPEÑO CHEDDAR BAGELS

I've never been one to opt for super crazy bagel flavors, but cheddar cheese and some jalapeños is just interesting enough to shake up my bagel baking every once in a while. You can add more jalapeños if you like it spicy, just make sure to drain the excess liquid well and take care to add a touch more flour so that the dough isn't too soft.

Yields 8 to 10 bagels

INGREDIENTS

2 teaspoons dry yeast

½ teaspoon sugar

1½ cups lukewarm water

4 cups + 3 tablespoons unbleached bread flour

2 teaspoons + pinch salt

1 heaping tablespoon + 2 teaspoons malt barley

½ cup grated Cheddar

⅓ cup chopped, pickled jalapeños

INSTRUCTIONS

Place the yeast and sugar in a small bowl or liquid measuring cup. Add the lukewarm water and stir gently to mix. Let stand 5 minutes.

Meanwhile, add the flour, 2 teaspoons salt, and 1 heaping tablespoon malt barley in a stand mixer fitted with a hook attachment.

Once the yeast-water mixture has started bubbling on top, add to mixer bowl and start mixing on low speed. Add the cheese and jalapeños and continue mixing. When the dough begins to come together, 3 to 4 minutes, raise speed to medium-low.

Keep mixing for another 5 to 7 minutes, until dough is elastic, shiny, and dense. Remove from bowl and allow to rest 1 minute.

Divide into 8 to 10 small sections. Each section should measure 3 to 4 ounces (use a food scale for precision), depending on how large you want your bagels.

Roll each section into a ball and place on a baking sheet lined with parchment paper or silicone baking mat. Cover for 10 to 15 minutes.

Shape your bagels: Roll each piece dough into a 3- to 4-inch rope, tapering ends just slightly. See pages 144–145 for shaping.

One at a time, take the ends of the rope and overlap them just slightly, pinch and then roll with the palm of your hands. If your shape isn't quite uniform, roll the other side of the bagel by placing your palm inside the middle and roll gently until desired shape.

Place rolled bagels back on the baking sheet lined with parchment paper or silicone baking mat and cover with plastic wrap. Place in the fridge 12 to 18 hours.

When ready to boil and bake, place a pizza stone on the top rack of your oven. Preheat the oven to 500°F. Allow pizza stone to sit in heated oven for 30 minutes.

Bring a wide pot of water to a low boil over medium-high heat. Add 2 teaspoons malt barley and a pinch of salt to the pot.

Do not start boiling your bagels until your oven has completely preheated, because once the bagels boil for 1 to 2 minutes, you want to get the bagels into the oven immediately. Also do not take the bagels out of the fridge too soon, or they may spread and lose their shape.

Once the water is boiling, reduce heat just slightly so it's a robust simmer. Add the puffed side of the bagel into the water first (flatter side should be up). After 30 to 60 seconds, flip the bagel using a spider and let sit another 30 to 60 seconds.

Using your spider once again, remove bagel from water, allow excess water to drip back into the pot, and place the bagel flatter side down into the oven directly onto the heated pizza stone. If you are going to add toppings, add them quickly as you put the bagel into the oven.

After 10 minutes, flip the bagels onto the other side.

Bake another 3 to 5 minutes depending on how crispy you want the outside of your bagel. Allow to cool and serve immediately.

HAVE WITH: GRAVLAX

Homemade bagels may be slightly complicated to make at home, but gravlax is not. Buy a good piece of fresh salmon and cure it for several days in a salt-sugar and herb mixture. People always think it's so impressive when I serve up some homemade gravlax, but it's easier than almost any task in the kitchen—it doesn't even require cooking. I also like serving gravlax with freshly fried latkes for Hanukkah and Passover. Note: this recipe makes a large amount of gravlax, but you can halve this recipe to make a smaller amount.

Yields 10 to 12 servings

INGREDIENTS

1 cup salt

2 cups sugar

2 teaspoons fresh black pepper

1 bunch of fresh dill, chopped

2 heaping tablespoons prepared coarse horseradish

2 tablespoons fresh lemon zest

1 piece of salmon (2 pounds), cut into two even pieces, skin left on

INSTRUCTIONS

Combine salt, sugar, black pepper, dill, horseradish, and lemon zest in a bowl.

Place one half of the salmon on a piece of plastic wrap, skin side down. Cover with three-quarters of the salt-sugar mixture. Yes, it will be a lot. Place the other piece of salmon on top, skin side up. Put remaining salt-sugar mixture on sides of salmon and on top of the other piece.

Wrap tightly in plastic wrap and place on a wire rack on top of a baking sheet.

Place in the fridge for 3 to 5 days. I prefer my gravlax to sit closer to 5 days, but you can eat it after 3 days. You will notice the fish releases liquid as the days progress. Feel free to drain.

When ready to serve, rinse off the salmon in cold water. Dry, remove skin, and then slice on the bias, cutting against the grain. Serve with bagels, cream cheese, slices of lemon, and other desired fixings.

BLUEBERRY BAGELS

If you like cinnamon raisin bagels, you will love these slightly sweet blueberry bagels. The color is beautiful and the taste is subtle, not overwhelming. It is perfect toasted and served simply with cream cheese or butter.

Yields 8 to 10 bagels

INGREDIENTS

2 teaspoons dry yeast

½ teaspoon sugar

1½ cups lukewarm water

4¼ cups unbleached bread flour

2 teaspoons + pinch salt

1 heaping tablespoon + 2 teaspoons malt barley

1 cup fresh blueberries

INSTRUCTIONS

Place the yeast and sugar in a small bowl or liquid measuring cup. Add the lukewarm water and stir gently to mix. Let stand 5 minutes.

Meanwhile, add 4 cups of the flour, 2 teaspoons salt, and 1 heaping tablespoon malt barley in a stand mixer fitted with a hook attachment.

Once the yeast-water mixture has started bubbling on top, add to bowl and start mixing on low speed. When the dough begins to come together, 3 to 4 minutes, raise speed to medium-low.

Toss the blueberries with remaining ¼ cup flour and add to dough. Keep mixing for another 5 to 7 minutes, until dough is elastic, shiny, and dense. Remove from bowl and allow to rest 1 minute.

Divide into 8 to 10 small sections. Each section should measure 3 to 4 ounces (use a food scale for precision), depending on how large you want your bagels.

Roll each section into a ball and place on a baking sheet lined with parchment paper or silicone baking mat. Cover for 10 to 15 minutes.

Shape your bagels: Roll each piece of dough into a 3- to 4-inch rope, tapering ends just slightly. See pages 144–145 for shaping.

One at a time, take the ends of the rope and overlap them just slightly, pinch and then roll with the palm of your hands. If your shape isn't quite uniform, roll the other side of the bagel by placing your palm inside the middle and roll gently until desired shape.

Place rolled bagels back on the baking sheet lined with parchment paper or silicone baking mat and cover with plastic wrap. Place in the fridge 12 to 18 hours.

When ready to boil and bake, place a pizza stone on the top rack of your oven. Preheat the oven to 500°F. Allow pizza stone to sit in heated oven for 30 minutes.

Bring a wide pot of water to a low boil over medium-high heat. Add 2 teaspoons malt barley and a pinch of salt to the pot.

Do not start boiling your bagels until your oven has completely preheated, because once the bagels boil for 1 to 2 minutes, you want to get the bagels into the oven immediately. Also do not take the bagels out of the fridge too soon, or they may spread and lose their shape.

Once the water is boiling, reduce heat just slightly so it's a robust simmer. Add the puffed side of the bagel into the water first (flatter side should be up). After 30 to 60 seconds, flip the bagel using a spider and let sit another 30 to 60 seconds.

Using your spider once again, remove bagel from water, allow excess water to drip back into the pot, and place the bagel flatter side down into the oven directly onto the heated pizza stone. If you are going to add toppings, add them quickly as you put the bagel into the oven.

After 10 minutes, flip the bagels onto the other side.

Bake another 3 to 5 minutes depending on how crispy you want the outside of your bagel. Allow to cool and serve immediately.

CINNAMON RAISIN BAGELS

Cinnamon raisin bagels were always a staple in my house, where bagels were practically their own food group for my brother Jon. I might opt to enjoy these cinnamon raisin bagels with butter rather than cream cheese.

Yields 8 to 10 bagels

INGREDIENTS

2 teaspoons dry yeast

½ teaspoon sugar

1½ cups lukewarm water

4 cups unbleached bread flour

2 teaspoons cinnamon

2 teaspoons + pinch salt

1 heaping tablespoon + 2 teaspoons malt barley

¾ cup raisins

INSTRUCTIONS

Place the yeast and sugar in a small bowl or liquid measuring cup. Add the lukewarm water and stir gently to mix. Let stand 5 minutes.

Meanwhile, add the flour, cinnamon, 2 teaspoons salt, and 1 heaping tablespoon malt barley in a stand mixer fitted with a hook attachment.

Once the yeast-water mixture has started bubbling on top, add to bowl and start mixing on low speed. Once the dough begins to come together, 3 to 4 minutes, add raisins, and raise speed to medium-low.

Keep mixing for another 5 to 7 minutes, until dough is elastic, shiny, and dense. Remove from bowl and allow to rest 1 minute.

Divide dough into 8 to 10 small sections. Each section should measure 3 to 4 ounces (use a food scale for precision), depending on how large you want your bagels.

Roll each section into a ball and place on a baking sheet lined with parchment paper or silicone baking mat. Cover for 10 to 15 minutes.

Shape your bagels: Roll each piece of dough into a 3- to 4-inch rope, tapering ends just slightly. See pages 144–145 for shaping.

One at a time, take the ends of the rope and overlap them just slightly, pinch and then roll with the palm of your hands. If your shape isn't quite uniform, roll the other side of the bagel by placing your palm inside the middle and roll gently until desired shape.

Place rolled bagels back on the baking sheet lined with parchment paper or silicone baking mat and cover with plastic wrap. Place in the fridge 12 to 18 hours.

When ready to boil and bake, place a pizza stone on the top rack of your oven. Preheat the oven to 500°F. Allow the pizza stone to sit in heated oven for 30 minutes.

Bring a wide pot of water to a low boil over medium-high heat. Add 2 teaspoons malt barley and a pinch of salt to the pot.

Do not start boiling your bagels until your oven has completely preheated, because once the bagels boil for 1 to 2 minutes, you want to get the bagels into the oven immediately. Also do not take the bagels out of the fridge too soon, or they may spread and lose their shape.

Once the water is boiling, reduce heat just slightly so it's a robust simmer. Add the puffed side of the bagel into the water first (flatter side should be up). After 30 to 60 seconds, flip the bagel using a spider and let sit another 30 to 60 seconds.

Using your spider once again, remove bagel from water, allow excess water to drip back into the pot, and place the bagel flatter side down into the oven directly onto the heated pizza stone. If you are going to add toppings, add them quickly as you put the bagel into the oven.

After 10 minutes, flip the bagels onto the other side.

Bake another 3 to 5 minutes depending on how crispy you want the outside of your bagel. Allow to cool and serve immediately.

LEFTOVER REMIX: PIZZA BAGELS

Pizza bagels are a beloved dish from my youth. We almost always had leftover bagels somewhere in the house, and so my favorite after-school treat was to make myself a pizza bagel. It's a fun activity, especially with kids, and it's even more delicious when made with homemade bagels.

Yields 2 to 4 servings

INGREDIENTS

2 leftover bagels

1 cup tomato sauce

2 cups grated mozzarella, Parmesan, or Cheddar (I like a mix of cheeses)

1 tablespoon chopped fresh basil

1–2 tablespoons pesto (optional)

Sliced tomato (optional)

Sliced olives (optional)

INSTRUCTIONS

Cut bagels in half. Spread small amount of tomato sauce on each bagel. Instead of tomato sauce, you can also use pesto.

Top with preferred cheeses and toppings.

Stick under broiler for 2 to 3 minutes, until cheese is bubbly and just brown. Serve immediately.

RUGELACH

While the origins of rugelach are European, the rugelach we know and love in the United States is very much an American invention. The use of cream cheese was not common in Europe, and once it was created in the U.S. in 1872, it slowly developed more and more applications in the American food landscape. It most famously gained popularity in the 1970s as an accompaniment to Sunday bagels. Cream cheese also made its way into various baked goods, like rugelach, where it adds a signature flakiness to the dough. In Israel, rugelach is more pastry-like, as it is made with yeast and laminated with a sugar syrup. They are often wonderfully gooey and would remind you of a European-style pastry. What is consistent between both versions is the crescent shape, since *rugelach* means "horn-shaped."

Rugelach was not a treat I grew up baking. In fact, Italian bakery cookies like rainbow cookies and white lace cookies were most beloved in my family. But as I expanded my Jewish baking repertoire over the years, I wanted to learn how to make these iconic Jewish cookies. I was grateful to get a personal lesson from Samantha Ferraro, a fellow blogger and Jewish food lover. Samantha's expert tips include using a pizza cutter to cut the dough into a perfect circle, and then into triangles before rolling up. It makes the job very easy.

HOW THE DOUGH SHOULD FEEL

The dough should be smooth, not crumbly and not sticky. Do not overmix.

CHILLING

The dough should chill for 1 to 2 hours in the fridge or overnight. If you are in a rush, pop the dough in the freezer for 30 minutes. If the dough gets too warm while working with it, place it back in the fridge for 5 to 10 minutes. The cookies are easiest to roll when the dough is still cold.

ESSENTIAL TOOLS

An *8 or 9-inch round cake pan or cutting ring* to cut out dough

Pizza cutter for cutting triangles

Small icing spatula for spreading various fillings

Silicone baking mat or parchment paper

Pastry brush for the egg wash

SHAPING RUGELACH

BASIC SWEET RUGELACH

Rugelach dough is quite simple to make. There are only a few ingredients that you will need to briefly mix before chilling for 1 to 2 hours or overnight. To keep the ruglelach delicate and flaky, the key is to not overmix.

Yields 2 ½ dozen cookies

INGREDIENTS

1 cup (2 sticks) unsalted butter, at room temperature

8 ounces full-fat cream cheese, at room temperature

¼ cup sugar

1 teaspoon vanilla

¼ teaspoon salt

2 cups unbleached all-purpose flour

1 egg, beaten (for glaze)

SUGGESTED FILLINGS:

¾ cup raspberry jam, Chocolate Filling (page 26), or other filling of your choice

INSTRUCTIONS

In a stand mixer fitted with a paddle attachment, beat the butter and cream cheese until smooth. Scrape down sides of bowl. Add the sugar, vanilla, and salt and beat until combined. You can also do this by hand.

Add the flour and mix just until dough comes together. Divide dough into four pieces. Wrap in plastic wrap and place in the fridge for 1 to 2 hours or up to 24 hours.

Preheat oven to 375°F.

Roll each piece of dough into a large circle. Using an 8- or 9-inch round, cut the dough into a perfect circle. I recommend using a pizza cutter for this task. See pages 164–165 for shaping.

Spread each circle of dough with a thin layer of filling, leaving ¼-inch border all around.

Using the pizza cutter, cut the dough into 8 even triangles. Starting at the longer end, roll up each triangle.

Place the point side down on a baking sheet lined with a parchment paper or silicone baking mat.

Brush each rugelach with beaten egg.

Bake for 16 to 18 minutes, until golden. Allow to cool on a wire rack.

BASIC SAVORY RUGELACH

This savory rugelach dough is just as simple to make as the sweet version. Add fresh herbs, garlic, tomato paste, harissa, or other oil-based flavorings to create a colorful and tasty savory pastry.

Yields 2½ dozen pastries

INGREDIENTS

1 cup (2 sticks) unsalted butter, at room temperature

8 ounces full-fat cream cheese, at room temperature

2 tablespoons sugar

¼ teaspoon salt

2 cups unbleached all-purpose flour

1 egg, beaten (for glaze)

SUGGESTED FILLINGS:

¾ cup Kale Basil Pesto (page 20) or other filling of your choice

INSTRUCTIONS

In a stand mixer fitted with a paddle attachment, beat the butter and cream cheese until smooth. Scrape down sides of bowl. Add the sugar and salt, and beat until combined. You can also do this by hand.

Add the flour and mix just until dough comes together. Divide dough into four pieces. Wrap in plastic wrap and place in the fridge for 1 to 2 hours or up to 24 hours.

Preheat oven to 375°F.

Roll each piece of dough into a large circle. Using an 8- or 9-inch round, cut the dough into a perfect circle. I recommend using a pizza cutter for this task. See pages 164–165 for shaping.

Spread each circle of dough with a thin layer of filling, leaving ¼-inch border all around.

Using the pizza cutter, cut the dough into 8 even triangles. Starting at the longer end, roll up each triangle.

Place the point side down on a baking sheet lined with parchment paper or silicone baking mat.

Brush each rugelach with beaten egg.

Bake for 16 to 18 minutes, until golden. Allow to cool on a wire rack.

PUMPKIN CHOCOLATE HAZELNUT RUGELACH

People often scoff at the combination of pumpkin and chocolate, but the flavors complement one another wonderfully. After all, pumpkin is a pretty neutral flavor—what most people consider "pumpkin" can be more accurately called pumpkin pie spice. The color of this rugelach is just stunning and the flavor features a sweetness that is just a tad different for your next tea party, brunch, or just because.

Yields 2 ½ dozen cookies

INGREDIENTS

1 cup (2 sticks) unsalted butter, at room temperature

8 ounces full-fat cream cheese, at room temperature

¼ cup sugar

¼ cup canned pumpkin

1 teaspoon vanilla

¼ teaspoon salt

2⅓ cups unbleached all-purpose flour, + an additional 1–2 tablespoons, if needed

¾ cup chocolate hazelnut spread

1 egg, beaten (for glaze)

INSTRUCTIONS

In a stand mixer fitted with a paddle attachment, beat the butter and cream cheese until smooth. Scrape down sides of bowl. Add the sugar, pumpkin, vanilla, and salt and beat until combined. You can also do this by hand.

Add the flour and mix just until dough comes together. Add up to 2 tablespoons of additional flour if dough is too sticky. Divide dough into four pieces. Wrap in plastic wrap and place in the fridge for 1 to 2 hours or up to 24 hours.

Preheat oven to 375°F.

Roll each piece of dough into a large circle. Using an 8- or 9-inch round, cut the dough into a perfect circle. I recommend using a pizza cutter for this task. See pages 164–165 for shaping.

Spread each circle of dough with 3 tablespoons of chocolate hazelnut spread in a thin layer, leaving ¼-inch border all around.

Using the pizza cutter, cut the dough into 8 even triangles. Starting at the longer end, roll up each triangle.

Place point side down on a baking sheet lined with parchment paper or silicone baking mat.

Brush each rugelach with beaten egg.

Bake for 16 to 18 minutes, until golden. Allow to cool on wire rack.

PEACH, ALMOND, AND WHITE CHOCOLATE RUGELACH

Peach and almond rugelach is a perfect summertime treat. If you can, pick up some fresh peach jam or preserves from your local farmers' market. If not, store-bought varieties will be perfectly delicious.

Yields 2½ dozen cookies

INGREDIENTS

1 cup (2 sticks) unsalted butter, at room temperature

8 ounces full-fat cream cheese, at room temperature

¼ cup sugar

1 teaspoon vanilla

¼ teaspoon salt

2 teaspoons orange zest

2 cups unbleached all-purpose flour

¾ cup peach jam

¼ cup chopped almonds

1 egg, beaten (for glaze)

1 cup white chocolate chips

1 tablespoon vegetable oil

INSTRUCTIONS

In a stand mixer fitted with a paddle attachment, beat the butter and cream cheese until smooth. Scrape down sides of bowl. Add the sugar, vanilla, salt, and orange zest and beat until combined. You can also do this by hand.

Add the flour and mix just until dough comes together. Divide the dough into four pieces. Wrap in plastic wrap and place in the fridge for 1 to 2 hours or up to 24 hours.

Preheat oven to 375°F.

Roll each piece of dough into a large circle. Using an 8- or 9-inch round, cut the dough into a perfect circle. I recommend using a pizza cutter for this task. See pages 164–165 for shaping.

Spread each circle of dough with 3 tablespoons of peach jam, leaving ¼-inch border all around. Sprinkle with 1 tablespoon of chopped almonds.

Using the pizza cutter, cut the dough into 8 even triangles. Starting at the longer end, roll up each triangle.

Place point side down on a baking sheet lined with parchment paper or silicone baking mat.

Brush each rugelach with beaten egg.

Bake for 16 to 18 minutes, until golden. Allow to cool on wire rack.

To make white chocolate drizzle, combine the white chocolate chips with vegetable oil in a microwave-safe bowl. Microwave for 30-second intervals, mixing in between with a small spatula, until completely melted and smooth. Drizzle white chocolate over top of rugelach. Allow to set.

RASPBERRY CHOCOLATE RUGELACH

Raspberry and chocolate are a perfect, classic combination for rugelach. You can use mini chocolate chips or finely chopped, good-quality dark chocolate to sprinkle on top of the raspberry jam layer. These are sweet and tart perfection.

Yields 2½ dozen cookies

INGREDIENTS

1 cup (2 sticks) unsalted butter, at room temperature

8 ounces full-fat cream cheese, at room temperature

¼ cup sugar

1 teaspoon vanilla

¼ teaspoon salt

2 cups unbleached all-purpose flour

½ cup dark chocolate chips or chunks

¾ cup raspberry jam

1 egg, beaten (for glaze)

INSTRUCTIONS

In a stand mixer fitted with a paddle attachment, beat the butter and cream cheese until smooth. Scrape down sides of bowl. Add the sugar, vanilla, and salt and beat until combined. You can also do this by hand.

Add the flour and mix just until dough comes together. Divide dough into four pieces. Wrap in plastic wrap and place in the fridge for 1 to 2 hours or up to 24 hours.

Preheat oven to 375°F.

Roll each piece of dough into a large circle. Using an 8- or 9-inch round, cut the dough into a perfect circle. I recommend using a pizza cutter for this task. See pages 164–165 for shaping.

Place the dark chocolate chips in a food processor fitted with a blade attachment and pulse until you have fine chocolate "crumbs."

Spread each circle of dough with approximately 3 tablespoons raspberry jam, leaving ¼-inch border all around. Top with a thin, even layer of chocolate crumbs.

Using the pizza cutter, cut the dough into 8 even triangles. Starting at the longer end, roll up each triangle.

Place the point side down on a baking sheet lined with parchment paper or a silicone baking mat.

Brush each rugelach with beaten egg.

Bake for 16 to 18 minutes, until golden. Allow to cool on wire rack.

CHOCOLATE PEPPERMINT RUGELACH

Every year during the holiday season, I crave connection to my Italian mom and her holiday cookie baking. Combining classic Christmas flavors with one of my favorite Jewish cookies has become my American Jewish compromise. Then again, who doesn't love the combination of dark chocolate and mint? I prefer using peppermint bark, but crushed up candy canes or mint candies are terrific choices.

Yields 2½ dozen cookies

INGREDIENTS

1 cup (2 sticks) unsalted butter, at room temperature

8 ounces full-fat cream cheese, at room temperature

¼ cup sugar

1 teaspoon vanilla

¼ teaspoon salt

2 cups unbleached all-purpose flour

1 cup (approximately 6 ounces) dark or semi-sweet chocolate chips

Pinch salt (optional)

3–4 ounces peppermint bark, + additional, for topping

1 egg, beaten (for glaze)

1 cup (approximately 6 ounces) white chocolate chips

1 tablespoon vegetable oil

INSTRUCTIONS

In a stand mixer fitted with a paddle attachment, beat the butter and cream cheese until smooth. Scrape down sides of bowl. Add the sugar, vanilla, and ¼ teaspoon salt and beat until combined. You can also do this by hand.

Add the flour and mix just until dough comes together. Divide the dough into four pieces. Wrap in plastic wrap and place in the fridge for 1 to 2 hours or up to 24 hours.

Preheat oven to 375°F.

Roll each piece of dough into a large circle. Using an 8- or 9-inch round, cut the dough into a perfect circle. I recommend using a pizza cutter for this task. See pages 164–165 for shaping.

In a microwave-safe bowl, heat the chocolate chips in 30-second intervals until smooth and melted, mixing in between with a small spatula, until completely melted and smooth. Add a pinch of salt to chocolate if desired.

Chop the peppermint bark into small pieces.

Spread each circle of dough with 3 tablespoons of chocolate in a thin layer, leaving ¼ inch-border all around. Sprinkle with chopped peppermint bark and press gently into chocolate.

Using the pizza cutter, cut the dough into 8 even triangles. Starting at the longer end, roll up each triangle.

continued

Place the point side down on a baking sheet lined with parchment paper or silicone baking mat.

Brush each rugelach with beaten egg.

Bake for 16 to 18 minutes, until golden. Allow to cool on wire rack.

To make white chocolate drizzle, combine white chocolate chips with vegetable oil in a microwave-safe bowl. Microwave for 30-second intervals, mixing in between with a small spatula, until completely melted and smooth.

Drizzle white chocolate over the top of rugelach. Top with additional peppermint bark. Allow to set.

PESTO PARMESAN RUGELACH

Pesto is a perfect filling for savory rugelach—it spreads easily and it subtly seasons the rugelach dough as it bakes. Add dried herbs, coarse sea salt, and extra Parmesan to the top for a touch more flavor and texture.

Yields 2 ½ dozen pastries

INGREDIENTS

1 cup (2 sticks) unsalted butter, at room temperature

8 ounces full-fat cream cheese, at room temperature

2 tablespoons sugar

¼ teaspoon salt

2 cups unbleached all-purpose flour

½–¾ cup pesto

¼ cup finely grated Parmesan

1 egg, beaten (for glaze)

1 teaspoon dried basil

¼ teaspoon coarse sea salt

INSTRUCTIONS

In a stand mixer fitted with a paddle attachment, beat the butter and cream cheese until smooth. Scrape down sides of bowl. Add the sugar and salt and beat until combined. You can also do this by hand.

Add the flour and mix just until dough comes together. Divide dough into four pieces. Wrap in plastic wrap and place in the fridge for 1 to 2 hours or up to 24 hours.

Preheat oven to 375°F.

Roll each piece of dough into a large circle. Using an 8- or 9-inch round, cut the dough into a perfect circle. I recommend using a pizza cutter for this task. See pages 164–165 for shaping.

Spread each circle of dough with 2 to 3 tablespoons pesto in a thin layer, leaving ¼-inch border all around. Sprinkle each circle with 1 tablespoon finely grated Parmesan. Press cheese gently into pesto.

Using the pizza cutter, cut the dough into 8 even triangles. Starting at the longer end, roll up each triangle.

Place the point side down on a baking sheet lined with parchment paper or silicone baking mat.

Brush each rugelach with beaten egg and top with dried basil and coarse sea salt.

Bake for 16 to 18 minutes, until golden. Allow to cool on wire rack.

SPICY PIZZA RUGELACH

The first thing that will strike you about this spicy pizza rugelach is the beautiful color. And then when you set your teeth into them, it's like taking that first bite of a great New York slice topped with a sprinkle of red pepper flakes.

Yields 2 ½ dozen pastries

INGREDIENTS

1 cup (2 sticks) unsalted butter, at room temperature

8 ounces full-fat cream cheese, at room temperature

2 tablespoons sugar

¼ teaspoon salt

2 tablespoons tomato paste

2 cups + 3 tablespoons unbleached all-purpose flour

½–¾ cup marinara or pizza sauce

½ cup shredded mozzarella

1 egg, beaten (for glaze)

1 teaspoon dried basil

1 teaspoon dried oregano

¼ teaspoon red pepper flakes

INSTRUCTIONS

In a stand mixer fitted with a paddle attachment, beat the butter and cream cheese until smooth. Scrape down sides of bowl. Add the sugar, salt, and tomato paste and beat until combined. You can also do this by hand.

Add the flour and mix just until dough comes together. Divide the dough into four pieces. Wrap in plastic wrap and place in the fridge for 1 to 2 hours or up to 24 hours.

Preheat oven to 375°F.

Roll each piece of dough into a large circle. Using an 8- or 9-inch round, cut dough into a perfect circle. I recommend using a pizza cutter for this task. See pages 164–165 for shaping.

Spread each circle of dough with 2 to 3 tablespoons of marinara sauce in a thin layer, leaving ¼-inch border all around. Sprinkle each circle with 2 tablespoons of shredded mozzarella and press gently into sauce.

Using the pizza cutter, cut the dough into 8 even triangles. Starting at the longer end, roll up each triangle.

Place the point side down on a baking sheet lined with parchment paper or silicone baking mat.

Brush each rugelach with beaten egg and sprinkle with dried basil, dried oregano, and red pepper flakes.

Bake for 16 to 18 minutes, until golden. Allow to cool on wire rack.

EVERYTHING BAGEL RUGELACH

I just adore these Everything Bagel Rugelach. They are crunchy, delicate, and a little sweet—the perfect treat for brunch or cocktails. If you like it spicy, make sure to add some crushed red pepper flakes to your Everything Bagel Topping (page 14).

Yields 2½ dozen pastries

INGREDIENTS

1 cup (2 sticks) unsalted butter, at room temperature

20 ounces full-fat cream cheese, at room temperature, divided

2 tablespoons sugar

¼ teaspoon salt

2 cups unbleached all-purpose flour

1 tablespoon lemon zest

1 tablespoon fresh chopped dill

Pinch sea salt

1 tablespoon Everything Bagel Topping (page 14), + additional 2 to 3 tablespoons, for topping

1 egg, beaten (for glaze)

INSTRUCTIONS

In a stand mixer fitted with a paddle attachment, beat the butter and 8 ounces of the cream cheese until smooth. Scrape down sides of bowl. Add the sugar and salt and beat until combined. You can also do this by hand.

Add the flour and mix just until dough comes together. Divide the dough into four pieces. Wrap in plastic wrap and place in the fridge for 1 hour or up to 24 hours.

Preheat oven to 375°F.

To make the filling, combine the remaining 12 ounces cream cheese with lemon zest, dill, and sea salt.

Roll each piece of dough into a large circle. Using an 8- or 9-inch round, cut dough into perfect circle. I recommend using a pizza cutter for this task. See pages 164–165 for shaping.

Spread each circle of dough with one-fourth of the cream cheese mixture in a thin layer, leaving ¼-inch border all around. Sprinkle each circle with ¾ teaspoon Everything Bagel Topping.

Using the pizza cutter, cut the dough into 8 even triangles. Starting at the longer end, roll up each triangle.

Place the point side down on a baking sheet lined with parchment paper or silicone baking mat.

Brush each rugelach with beaten egg and top with additional everything bagel topping.

Bake for 16 to 18 minutes, until golden. Allow to cool on wire rack.

HARISSA AND GOAT CHEESE RUGELACH

Harissa is a classic North African pepper condiment with a pesto-like consistency that spreads easily. Although it is not difficult to make a homemade version of harissa, it has become pretty easy to find at the supermarket (different brands vary in spiciness; try a few to see what you like). Topped with creamy goat cheese to balance the heat, this rugelach is a perfect match between Ashkenazi pastries and Middle Eastern flavors.

Yields 2½ dozen pastries

INGREDIENTS

1 cup (2 sticks) unsalted butter, at room temperature

8 ounces full-fat cream cheese, at room temperature

2 tablespoons sugar

¼ teaspoon salt

2 cups unbleached all-purpose flour

½–¾ cup harissa

2 ounces goat cheese

1 egg, beaten (for glaze)

INSTRUCTIONS

In a stand mixer fitted with a paddle attachment, beat the butter and cream cheese until smooth. Scrape down sides of bowl. Add the sugar and salt and beat until combined. You can also do this by hand.

Add the flour and mix just until dough comes together. Divide the dough into four pieces. Wrap in plastic wrap and place in the fridge for 1 to 2 hours or up to 24 hours.

Preheat oven to 375°F.

Roll each piece of dough into a large circle. Using an 8- or 9-inch round, cut the dough into a perfect circle. I recommend using a pizza cutter for this task. See pages 164–165 for shaping.

Spread each circle of dough with 2 to 3 tablespoons harissa in a thin layer, leaving ¼-inch border all around. Sprinkle ½ ounce of goat cheese on each circle, and use a small spatula to spread goat cheese gently into harissa.

Using the pizza cutter, cut the dough into 8 even triangles. Starting at the longer end, roll up each triangle.

Place the point side down on a baking sheet lined with parchment paper or silicone baking mat.

Brush each rugelach with beaten egg.

Bake for 16 to 18 minutes, until golden. Allow to cool on wire rack.

HAMANTASCHEN

There is a Jewish saying you are probably familiar with that goes, "They tried to kill us, we survived, let's eat." And in the case of Purim, it's fairly accurate: Haman, a powerful advisor in the royal court of ancient Persia, was planning to kill all the Jews in the empire. But those plans were thwarted with the feminist twist when Queen Esther, using her intellect and feminine prowess, helped the Jews survive. The hamantaschen itself is supposed to be a symbolic treat that is said to resemble the three corners of the hat worn by Haman, the villain of the Purim story.

More accurately, triangle-shaped treats filled with poppy seed, also known as *mohn*, were enjoyed in 18th century Germany. The treats already sounded like Haman (*mohn*) and so they were adopted by the Jews as a treat to celebrate Purim.

Hamantaschen have not traditionally been the most coveted of Jewish treats. The traditional European recipe uses yeast and a heavy flour ratio, which yields a thick cookie that can be crumbly and quite dry. These were the only version of hamantaschen I knew growing up, and so I had little desire to make them. And then I met Rachel and Susan Korycan.

Susan was a Catholic gal from Ohio who met a nice Jewish boy at a law school party, converted to Judaism, and got married. They had a beautiful daughter, my friend Rachel, and raised her proud and Jewish in Akron, Ohio. Susan was an avid baker, and like me, found that traditional hamantaschen left something to be desired. She did not have a family recipe or Jewish mother to confer with on hamantaschen baking, and so she did what a good Midwest baker does: She looked to her Betty Crocker Cookbook for inspiration. Susan's version of hamantaschen relied on a soft, butter dough which was moister, chewier, and even made shaping hamantaschen easier. My hamantaschen consumption and baking was changed forever.

HOW THE DOUGH SHOULD FEEL

The dough should be firm, not sticky, and easily shapeable.

CHILLING

You can chill the dough for 1 hour or overnight.

ESSENTIAL TOOLS

You will need something round to cut out the cookies, most ideally a **round cookie cutter** or biscuit cutter. You can also use the top of a mason jar or a regular drinking glass.

> **Rolling pin**
>
> **Silicone baking mat** or parchment paper

SPECIAL NOTES

Hamantaschen are notorious for opening up while baking and not keeping their shape. For this reason, I recommend filling and shaping your cookies, and then popping them into the freezer for 10 minutes before baking. This will ensure they maintain their shape and don't explode during baking.

SHAPING HAMANTASCHEN

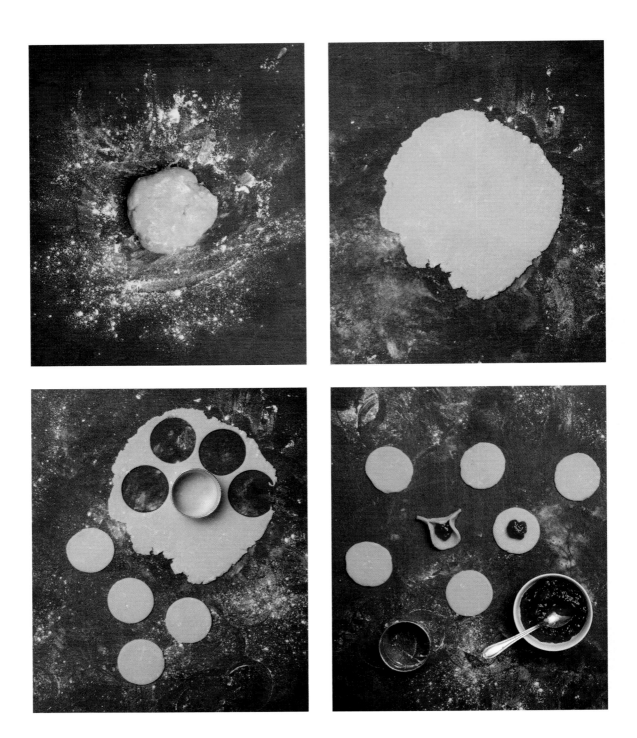

BASIC SWEET HAMANTASCHEN

Every year I get questions about what hamantaschen recipe I use and how best to shape it. I love this recipe because it is simple and the results are absolutely delicious. Make sure to pop your shaped hamantaschen in the freezer for 10 minutes before baking, and you will never have a hamantaschen explosion.

Yields 1½ to 2 dozen cookies

INGREDIENTS

½ cup (1 stick) unsalted butter (or margarine), at room temperature

¾ cup granulated sugar

1 egg

1 tablespoon whole milk (or almond milk)

1 teaspoon vanilla

1½ cups unbleached all-purpose flour, + additional 1–2 tablespoons, if needed

¼ teaspoon baking powder

¼ teaspoon salt

1 cup jam of your choice, for filling

INSTRUCTIONS

In a stand mixer fitted with whisk attachment or by hand, beat the butter and sugar together until smooth. Add the egg, milk, and vanilla and beat until mixed thoroughly.

In a separate bowl, mix the flour, baking powder, and salt. Add the dry mixture to the wet mixture until incorporated. If the dough seems too wet still, add additional flour 1 tablespoon at a time.

Chill dough for at least 1 hour or up to 24 hours.

Lightly dust work surface with flour. Split dough into two parts. Roll out first piece of dough to about ¼-inch thick. Using a round cookie cutter, cut out and place the dough onto a baking sheet lined with parchment paper or silicone baking mat. To keep the dough from sticking to your cutter, dip cookie cutter in flour.

Fill each round with ½ teaspoon jam. Pinch up the dough to form a triangle. Pinch dough very tightly to ensure they do not open. Place cookies on a baking sheet lined with parchment paper or silicone baking mat. See pages 190–191 for shaping.

Repeat with remaining dough, adding scraps each time back into dough. If dough becomes too soft, pop into the freezer for 5 minutes to chill slightly.

Preheat oven to 400°F.

Place cookies in freezer for 10 minutes. This step will ensure the cookies don't spread too much or open during the process of baking.

Bake for 8 to 9 minutes, or until cookies are just golden around the edges. Allow to cool completely on a wire rack.

BASIC SAVORY HAMANTASCHEN

Savory hamantaschen have gained wide popularity in recent years, and I have seen every variety from BBQ brisket to jalapeño cheddar flavored. This simple, more savory dough lends itself well to vegetable and cheese fillings, my favorite savory varieties.

Yields 1½ to 2 dozen pastries

INGREDIENTS

½ cup (1 stick) unsalted butter (or margarine)

½ cup granulated sugar

1 egg

1 tablespoon whole or 2% milk (or almond milk)

1 teaspoon vanilla

1½ cups unbleached all-purpose flour, + additional 1–2 tablespoons, if needed

¼ teaspoon baking powder

¼ teaspoon salt

Choice of 1 cup Savory Onion Jam (page 23), shredded cheese, or mashed potatoes, for filling

INSTRUCTIONS

In a stand mixer fitted with whisk attachment or by hand, beat the butter and sugar together until smooth. Add the egg, milk, and vanilla and beat until mixed thoroughly.

In a separate bowl, mix the flour, baking powder, and salt. Add the dry mixture to the wet mixture until incorporated. If the dough seems too wet still, add additional flour 1 tablespoon at a time.

Chill dough for at least 1 hour or up to 24 hours.

Lightly dust work surface with flour. Split dough into two parts. Roll out first piece of dough to about ¼-inch thick. Using a round cookie cutter, cut out and place the dough onto a baking sheet lined with parchment paper or silicone baking mat. To keep the dough from sticking to your cutter, dip cookie cutter in flour.

Fill each round with ½ teaspoon filling. Pinch up the dough to form a triangle. Pinch dough very tightly to ensure they do not open. Place cookies on a baking sheet lined with parchment paper or silicone baking mat. See pages 190–191 for shaping.

Repeat with remaining dough, adding scraps each time back into dough. If dough becomes too soft, pop into the freezer for 5 minutes to chill slightly.

Preheat oven to 400°F.

Place cookies in freezer for 10 minutes. This step will ensure the cookies don't spread too much or open during the process of baking.

Bake for 8 to 9 minutes, or until cookies are just golden around the edges. Allow to cool completely on a wire rack.

CHOCOLATE DIPPED SPRINKLES HAMANTASCHEN

I love sprinkles, and I love old-school style bakery cookies that are delicately dipped in chocolate and topped with a colorful portion of sprinkles. These hamantaschen are as beautiful to look at as they are delicious to eat. I prefer to use raspberry or strawberry jam paired with the chocolate, but you could use any filling you like including apricot jam, chocolate hazelnut spread, cream cheese filling, or even marshmallow fluff.

Yields 1½ to 2 dozen cookies

INGREDIENTS

½ cup (1 stick) unsalted butter (or margarine)

¾ cup granulated sugar

1 egg

1 tablespoon milk (or almond milk)

1 teaspoon vanilla

1½ cups unbleached all-purpose flour, + additional 1–2 tablespoons, if needed

¼ teaspoon baking powder

¼ teaspoon salt

3 tablespoons raspberry jam

1 cup (about 6 ounces) semi-sweet or dark chocolate chips

1 tablespoon vegetable oil

¼–½ cup colorful sprinkles

INSTRUCTIONS

In a stand mixer fitted with whisk attachment or by hand, beat the butter and sugar together until smooth. Add the egg, milk, and vanilla and beat until mixed thoroughly.

In a separate bowl, mix the flour, baking powder, and salt. Add the dry mixture to the wet mixture until incorporated. If the dough seems too wet still, add additional flour 1 tablespoon at a time.

Chill dough for at least 1 hour or up to 24 hours.

Lightly dust work surface with flour. Split dough into two parts. Roll out first piece of dough to about ¼-inch thick. Using a round cookie cutter, cut out and place the dough onto a baking sheet lined with parchment paper or silicone baking mat. To keep the dough from sticking to your cutter, dip cookie cutter in flour.

Fill each round with ½ teaspoon raspberry jam. Pinch up the dough to form a triangle. Pinch dough very tightly to ensure they do not open. Place cookies on a baking sheet lined with parchment paper or silicone baking mat. See pages 190–191 for shaping.

Repeat with remaining dough, adding scraps each time back into dough. If dough becomes too soft, pop into the freezer for 5 minutes to chill slightly.

Preheat oven to 400°F.

continued

Place cookies in freezer for 10 minutes. This step will ensure the cookies don't spread too much or open during the process of baking.

Bake for 8 to 9 minutes, or until cookies are just golden around the edges. Allow to cool completely on a wire rack.

Combine the chocolate chips with the vegetable oil in a microwave-safe bowl. Microwave for 30-second intervals, mixing in between with a small spatula, until completely melted and smooth.

Partly dip each cookie into the melted chocolate. Place the cookies on a parchment-lined baking sheet. Top with a generous amount of colored sprinkles. Allow to set completely.

S'MORES HAMANTASCHEN

Purim is all about joy and celebration, and I can't think of anything more joyous than a marshmallow-filled chocolate-dipped hamantaschen topped with graham cracker crumbs. Instead of mini marshmallows baked into the cookies, you could substitute marshmallow fluff. This variation is one of my husband's absolute favorites (and mine too).

Yields 1½ to 2 dozen cookies

INGREDIENTS

½ cup (1 stick) unsalted butter (or margarine)

¾ cup granulated sugar

1 egg

1 tablespoon whole or 2% milk (or almond milk)

1 teaspoon vanilla

1½ cups unbleached all-purpose flour, + additional 1–2 tablespoons, if needed

¼ teaspoon baking powder

¼ teaspoon salt

3 tablespoons chocolate hazelnut spread

18–24 mini marshmallows

1 cup (approximately 6 ounces) semi-sweet chocolate chips

1 tablespoon vegetable oil

6 graham crackers, crushed

INSTRUCTIONS

In a stand mixer fitted with whisk attachment or by hand, beat the butter and sugar together until smooth. Add the egg, milk, and vanilla and beat until mixed thoroughly.

In a separate bowl, mix the flour, baking powder, and salt. Add the dry mixture to the wet mixture until incorporated. If the dough seems too wet still, add additional flour 1 tablespoon at a time.

Chill dough for at least 1 hour or up to 24 hours.

Lightly dust work surface with flour. Split dough into two parts. Roll out first piece of dough to about ¼-inch thick. Using a round cookie cutter, cut out and place the dough onto a baking sheet lined with parchment paper or silicone baking mat. To keep the dough from sticking to your cutter, dip cookie cutter in flour.

Fill each round with ½ teaspoon chocolate hazelnut spread and a mini marshmallow. Pinch up the dough to form a triangle. Pinch dough very tightly to ensure they do not open. Place cookies on a baking sheet lined with parchment or a silicone baking mat. See pages 190–191 for shaping.

Repeat with remaining dough, putting scraps back into dough 3 or 4 times until all the dough has been used. If dough becomes too soft, pop into the freezer for 5 minutes to chill slightly.

Preheat oven to 400°F.

continued

Place cookies in freezer for 10 minutes. This step will ensure the cookies don't spread too much or open during the process of baking.

Bake for 8 to 9 minutes, or until cookies are just golden around the edges. Allow to cool completely on a wire rack.

Combine the chocolate chips with the vegetable oil in a microwave-safe bowl. Microwave for 30 second intervals, mixing in between with a small spatula, until completely melted and smooth.

Partly dip each cookie into the melted chocolate. Place cookie on parchment-lined baking sheet. Sprinkle graham cracker cookie crumbs on top.

CHOCOLATE CHIP COOKIE HAMANTASCHEN

The fun of hamantaschen is usually in the creative fillings. But these hamantaschen put the fun in the dough itself, turning the traditional cookie into a chocolate chip cookie hybrid. You can still have fun with the fillings—try chocolate hazelnut spread, cookie butter, or dulce de leche.

Yields 1½ to 2 dozen cookies

INGREDIENTS

FOR THE DOUGH:

½ cup (1 stick) unsalted butter (or margarine), at room temperature

½ cup granulated sugar

¼ cup brown sugar, lightly packed

1 egg

1 tablespoon whole or 2% milk (or almond milk)

1 teaspoon vanilla extract

1¼ cups + 2 tablespoons all-purpose flour

¼ teaspoon baking powder

¼ teaspoon salt

¼ cup mini chocolate chips

FILLING SUGGESTIONS:

1–1½ cups chocolate hazelnut spread

1–1½ cups dulce de leche

1–1½ cups cookie butter

INSTRUCTIONS

In a stand mixer fitted with whisk attachment or by hand, beat the butter and sugars together until smooth. Add the egg, milk, and vanilla until mixed thoroughly.

In a separate bowl, sift together the flour, baking powder, and salt. Add the dry mixture to the wet mixture and mix until incorporated. Fold in the chocolate chips.

Chill the dough for at least 1 hour or up to 24 hours.

Preheat the oven to 400°F.

Dust your work surface with flour to keep the dough from sticking. I like to cut the dough in half and roll out in batches. Roll out the dough to ¼- to ½-inch thick. Using a round cookie cutter, cut out and place the dough onto a baking sheet lined with parchment paper or silicone baking mat. To keep the dough from sticking to your cutter, dip cookie cutter in flour.

Fill each round with ½ teaspoon of your choice of chocolate hazelnut spread, dulce de leche, or cookie butter. Pinch up the dough to form a triangle. Pinch dough very tightly to ensure they do not open. Place cookies on a baking sheet lined with parchment or a silicone baking mat. See pages 190–191 for shaping.

Repeat with remaining dough, putting scraps back into dough 3 or 4 times until all the dough has been used. If dough becomes too soft, pop into the freezer for 5 minutes to chill slightly.

Place cookies in freezer for 10 minutes. This step will ensure the cookies don't spread too much or open during the process of baking.

Bake for 8 to 9 minutes, or until cookies are just golden around the edges. Allow to cool completely on a wire rack.

TRIPLE CHOCOLATE HAMANTASCHEN

This cookie is beautiful, decadent, and perfect for the chocolate lover in your life. Make sure to use a good quality cocoa powder.

Yields 1½ to 2 dozen cookies

INGREDIENTS

½ cup (1 stick) unsalted butter (or margarine)

¾ cup granulated sugar

1 egg

1 tablespoon whole or 2% milk (or almond milk)

1 teaspoon vanilla

1¼ cups + 2 tablespoons all-purpose flour

¼ teaspoon baking powder

1 tablespoon cocoa powder

¼ teaspoon cinnamon

¼ teaspoon salt

3 tablespoons chocolate hazelnut spread

½ cup (about 3 ounces) white chocolate chips

2 teaspoons vegetable oil

INSTRUCTIONS

In a stand mixer fitted with whisk attachment or by hand, beat the butter and sugar together until smooth. Add the egg, milk, and vanilla and beat until mixed thoroughly.

In a separate bowl, mix the flour, baking powder, cocoa powder, cinnamon, and salt. Add the dry mixture to the wet mixture until incorporated. If the dough seems too wet still, add additional flour 1 tablespoon at a time.

Chill the dough for at least 1 hour or up to 24 hours.

Preheat the oven to 400°F.

Dust your work surface with flour to keep the dough from sticking. I like to cut dough in half and roll out in batches. Roll out the dough to ¼- to ½-inch thick. Using a round cookie cutter, cut out and place the dough onto a baking sheet lined with parchment paper or silicone baking mat. To keep the dough from sticking to your cutter, dip cookie cutter in flour.

Fill each round with ½ teaspoon of chocolate hazelnut spread. Pinch up the dough to form a triangle. Pinch dough very tightly to ensure they do not open. Place cookies on a baking sheet lined with parchment or a silicone baking mat. See pages 190–191 for shaping.

Repeat with remaining dough, putting scraps back into dough 3 or 4 times until all the dough has been used. If dough becomes too soft, pop into the freezer for 5 minutes to chill slightly.

Place cookies in freezer for 10 minutes. This step will ensure the cookies don't spread too much or open during the process of baking.

Bake for 8 to 9 minutes, or until cookies are just golden around the edges. Allow to cool completely on a wire rack.

To make white chocolate drizzle, place the white chocolate and vegetable oil in a small glass bowl. Heat in the microwave at 30-second intervals until melted. Mix until completely smooth.

Use a fork or a small plastic squeeze bottle to drizzle white chocolate sauce back and forth over cookies. Allow to dry completely on a cooling rack before serving or packaging.

COCONUT CHEESECAKE HAMANTASCHEN

Creamy coconut cheese filling is an unexpected hamantaschen flavor, but it's absolutely delicious. I like adding additional coconut flakes to the top after I have folded the cookie so that, as it bakes, there is just a touch of toasted coconut peeking out on top.

Yields 1½ to 2 dozen cookies

INGREDIENTS

FOR THE DOUGH:

½ cup (1 stick) unsalted butter (or margarine)

¾ cup granulated sugar

1 egg

1 tablespoon whole or 2% milk (or almond milk)

1 teaspoon vanilla

1½ cups unbleached all-purpose flour, + 1–2 additional tablespoons, if needed

¼ teaspoon baking powder

¼ teaspoon salt

FOR THE FILLING:

8 ounces cream cheese, at room temperature

2 tablespoons sugar

¼ cup heavy cream or full-fat coconut milk

1 teaspoon vanilla

¼ cup shredded coconut, + additional, for topping

INSTRUCTIONS

For the dough: In a stand mixer fitted with whisk attachment or by hand, beat the butter and sugar together until smooth. Add the egg, milk, and vanilla and beat until mixed thoroughly.

In a separate bowl, mix the flour, baking powder, and salt. Add the dry mixture to the wet mixture until incorporated. If the dough seems too wet still, add additional flour 1 tablespoon at a time.

Chill the dough for at least 1 hour or up to 24 hours.

To make the filling: Beat the cream cheese and sugar together. Add the heavy cream, vanilla, and shredded coconut until combined.

Dust your work surface with flour to keep the dough from sticking. I like to cut dough in half and roll out in batches. Roll out the dough to ¼- to ½-inch thick. Using a round cookie cutter, cut out and place the dough onto a baking sheet lined with parchment paper or silicone baking mat. To keep the dough from sticking to your cutter, dip cookie cutter in flour.

Fill each round with ½ teaspoon cream cheese filling. Pinch up the dough to form a triangle. Pinch dough very tightly to ensure they do not open. Top cookies with additional shredded coconut if desired. Place cookies on a baking sheet lined with parchment or a silicone baking mat. See pages 190–191 for shaping.

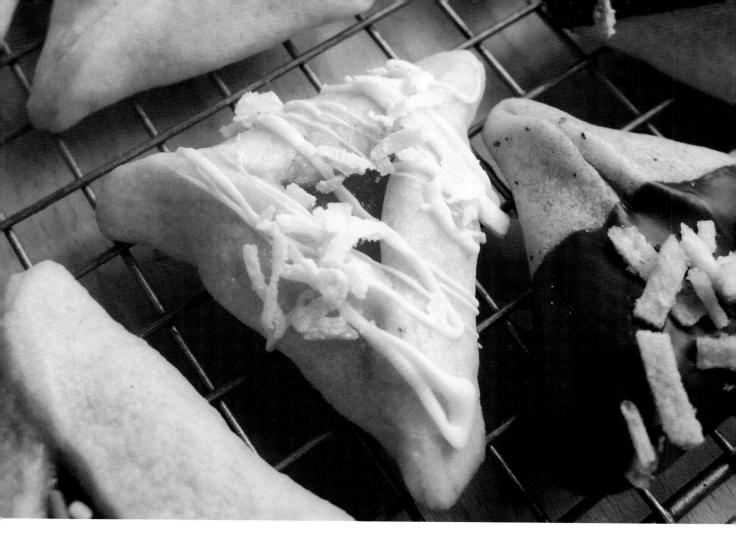

Repeat with remaining dough, putting scraps back into dough 3 or 4 times until all the dough has been used. If dough becomes too soft, pop into the freezer for 5 minutes to chill slightly.

Preheat oven to 400°F.

Place cookies in freezer for 10 minutes. This step will ensure the cookies don't spread too much or open during the process of baking.

Bake for 8 to 9 minutes, or until cookies are just golden around the edges. Allow to cool completely on a wire rack.

BRIE AND HERB HAMANTASCHEN

In the past ten years or so, savory varieties of hamantaschen have become more commonplace as home bakers, bloggers, and chefs alike have branched out way beyond traditional poppy seed and prune hamantaschen. While sweet hamantaschen are still my favorite, I also love these savory herb and melted Brie hamantaschen. They are simple but scrumptious.

Yields 1½ to 2 dozen pastries

INGREDIENTS

½ cup (1 stick) unsalted butter (or margarine)

¾ cup granulated sugar

1 egg

1 tablespoon whole or 2% milk (or almond milk)

1½ cups unbleached all-purpose flour, + additional 1–2 tablespoons, if needed

¼ teaspoon baking powder

¼ teaspoon salt

2 teaspoons herbes de Provence (or other dried herbs)

3–4 ounces Brie

INSTRUCTIONS

In a stand mixer fitted with whisk attachment or by hand, beat the butter and sugar together until smooth Add the egg and milk and beat until mixed thoroughly.

In a separate bowl, mix the flour, baking powder, salt, and herbes de Provence. Add the dry mixture to the wet mixture until incorporated. If the dough seems too wet still, add additional flour 1 tablespoon at a time.

Chill the dough for at least 1 hour or up to 24 hours.

Dust your work surface with flour to keep the dough from sticking. I like to cut dough in half and roll out in batches. Roll out the dough to ¼- to ½-inch thick. Using a round cookie cutter, cut out and place the dough onto a baking sheet lined with parchment paper or silicone baking mat. To keep the dough from sticking to your cutter, dip cookie cutter in flour.

Remove the rind on the Brie, and place a small piece of Brie into the center of each round. Pinch up the circle of dough to form a triangle. Pinch dough very tightly to ensure they do not open. Place pastries on a baking sheet lined with parchment paper or silicone baking mat. Repeat with the remaining dough, putting scraps back into dough 3 or 4 times until all dough has been used.

Preheat oven to 400°F.

Place pastries in freezer for 10 minutes. This step will ensure the pastries don't spread too much or open during the process of baking.

Bake for 8 to 9 minutes, or until pastries are just golden around the edges. Allow to cool completely on a wire rack.

ONION JAM AND GOAT CHEESE HAMANTASCHEN

These hamantaschen are a nice mix between sweet and savory. The onion jam brings a slight sweetness and the goat cheese adds tang and creaminess. If you want to make a nondairy version of hamantaschen, you can leave out the goat cheese.

Yields 1½ to 2 dozen pastries

INGREDIENTS

½ cup (1 stick) unsalted butter (or margarine)

¾ cup granulated sugar

1 egg

1 tablespoon whole or 2% milk (or almond milk)

1½ cups unbleached all-purpose flour, + an additional 1–2 tablespoons, if needed

¼ teaspoon baking powder

¼ teaspoon salt

3 tablespoons Savory Onion Jam (page 23)

3–4 ounces goat cheese

INSTRUCTIONS

In a stand mixer fitted with whisk attachment or by hand, beat the butter and sugar together until smooth Add the egg and milk and beat until mixed thoroughly.

In a separate bowl, mix the flour, baking powder, and salt. Add the dry mixture to the wet mixture until incorporated. If dough seems too wet still, add additional flour 1 tablespoon at a time.

Chill dough for at least 1 hour or up to 24 hours.

Dust your work surface with flour to keep the dough from sticking. I like to cut dough in half and roll out in batches. Roll out the dough to ¼- to ½-inch thick. Using a round cookie cutter, cut out and place the dough onto a baking sheet lined with parchment paper or silicone baking mat. To keep the dough from sticking to your cutter, dip cookie cutter in flour.

Fill each round with ½ teaspoon Savory Onion Jam and a small piece of goat cheese. Pinch up the circle of dough to form a triangle. Pinch dough very tightly to ensure they do not open. See folding instructions on pages 190–191. Place pastries on a baking sheet lined with parchment paper or silicone baking mat. Repeat with the remaining dough, putting scraps back into dough 3 or 4 times until all dough has been used.

Preheat oven to 400°F.

Place pastries in freezer for 10 minutes. This step will ensure the pastries don't spread too much or open during the process of baking.

Bake for 8 to 9 minutes, or until pastries are just golden around the edges. Allow to cool completely on a wire rack.

RYE CRUST HAMANTASCHEN WITH GRAPE JELLY

When people think of rye they probably exclusively refer to rye bread or other Scandinavian or European breads. But rye flour goes wonderfully into baked goods like pie crust, challah dough, and yes, hamantaschen too. My husband, who detests rye bread with seeds, was skeptical about this cookie, but he was easily won over. The slightly earthy, sour taste of the rye pairs perfectly with sweet grape jelly.

Yields 1½ to 2 dozen pastries

INGREDIENTS

½ cup (1 stick) unsalted butter (or margarine)

¾ cup sugar

1 egg

1 tablespoon whole or 2% milk (or almond milk)

1 teaspoon vanilla

¾ cup rye flour

½ cup unbleached all-purpose flour, + more

¼ teaspoon baking powder

½ teaspoon cinnamon

¼ teaspoon salt

3 tablespoons grape jelly

Caraway seeds, for topping (optional)

INSTRUCTIONS

In a stand mixer fitted with whisk attachment or by hand, beat the butter and sugar together until smooth. Add the egg, milk, and vanilla and beat until mixed thoroughly.

In a separate bowl, sift together the flours, baking powder, cinnamon, and salt. Add the dry mixture to the wet mixture and mix until incorporated.

Chill dough for at least 1 hour or up to 24 hours.

Preheat the oven to 400°F.

Dust your work surface with flour to keep the dough from sticking. I like to cut the dough in half and roll out in batches. Roll out the dough to ¼- to ½-inch thick. Using a round cookie cutter, cut out and place the dough onto a baking sheet lined with parchment paper or silicone baking mat. To keep the dough from sticking to your cutter, dip cookie cutter in flour.

Fill each round with ½ teaspoon grape jelly. Pinch up the circle of dough to form a triangle. Pinch dough very tightly to ensure they do not open. See folding instructions on pages 190–191. Top with a sprinkle of caraway seeds if desired. Place pastries on a baking sheet lined with parchment paper or silicone baking mat. Repeat with the remaining dough, putting scraps back into dough 3 or 4 times until all dough has been used.

Place entire baking sheet into the freezer for 5 minutes before baking (or place in the fridge for 10 to 15 minutes). This will ensure the pastries don't fall apart while baking.

Bake for 8 to 9 minutes, or until pastries are just golden around the edges. Allow to cool completely on a wire rack.

PITA BREAD

You may be thinking: Pita isn't a Jewish bread. Although it's true that pita isn't an Eastern European Jewish bread, it is consumed and beloved throughout the Middle East and is a staple for Israeli cuisine.

I remember the first time I had fresh pita in Israel, and like my first taste of real hummus (also in Israel), I was blown away by its completely different flavor and texture. Fluffy, warm pita straight from the oven is nothing like the flat, packaged pita you buy in the store. Another secret: Pita is so easy to make, so much easier than I ever thought. One day I just decided to try to make it, and I have been addicted ever since.

You can serve pita in lieu of sandwich bread, or you can stuff it with shawarma, chicken cutlets, eggplant, or salad. My favorite way to enjoy pita is with some good dips.

HOW THE DOUGH SHOULD FEEL

The dough should not be as firm as a bagel dough, but it should not be soft like a challah or babka dough, either. It should be smooth, bounce back slightly when touched, and not be sticky.

FLOUR

I recommend using a combination of two parts unbleached all-purpose flour and one part whole-wheat flour. You can use all white flour if you prefer.

RISING

The rise for pita is relatively short. You can wake up one day and decide to make pita, and have it ready well in time for lunch. Like challah, you must allow for a second rise, as the second rise will ensure that the pita "puffs up" to create the desirable pocket inside.

ESSENTIAL TOOLS

Pizza stone for baking

Tongs

SHAPING PITA

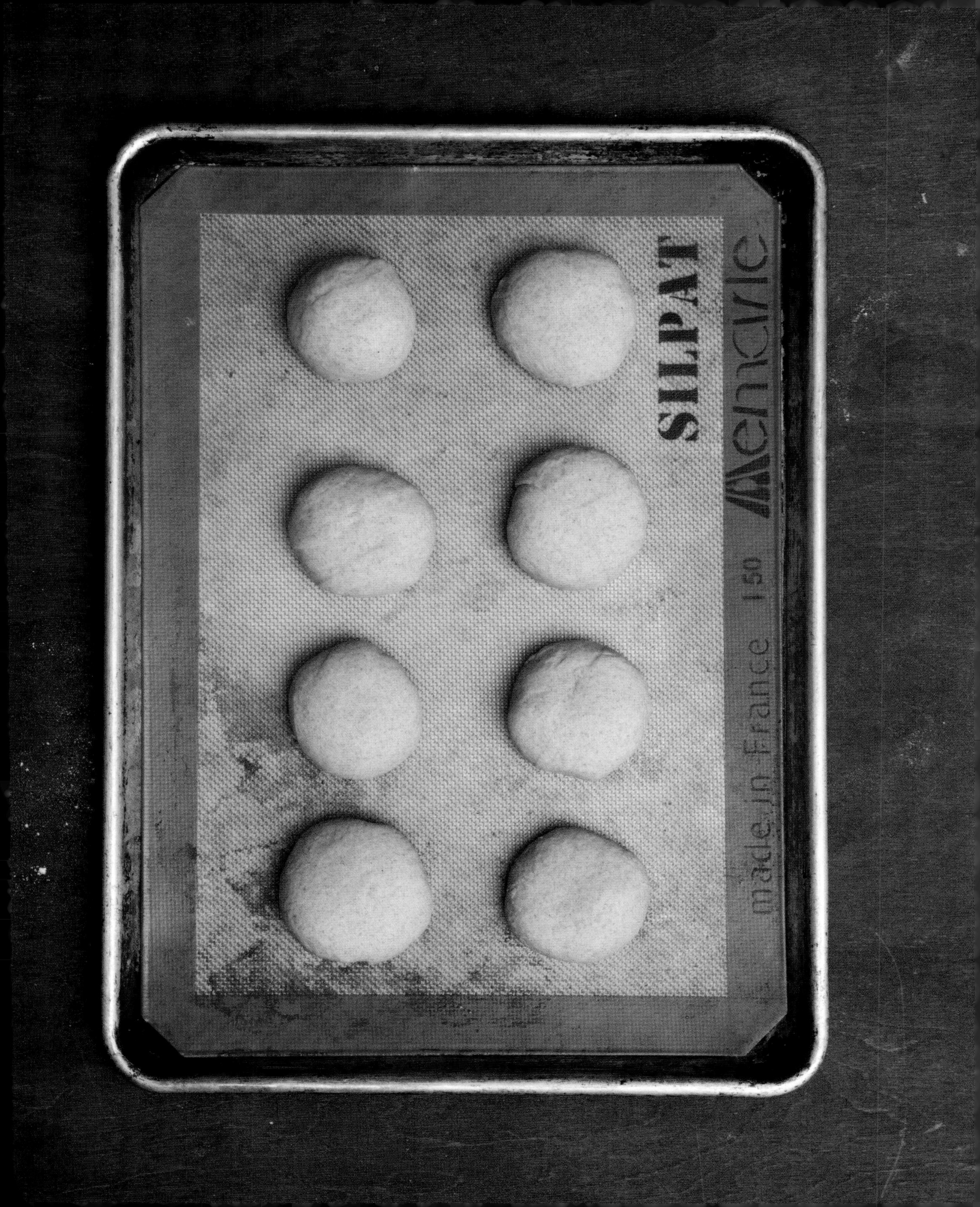
SILPAT
made in France
150

BASIC PITA BREAD

Once you make your own pita bread, you will never go back to store-bought. It's a relatively quick bread to make from scratch since it only requires 1½ to 2½ hours of rising. And there is nothing quite as gratifying as watching the pita rise in the oven and puff up to form its coveted pocket.

Yields 6 to 8 pieces

INGREDIENTS

2 teaspoons yeast

½ teaspoon sugar

1 cup + 1 tablespoon lukewarm water

2 cups all-purpose flour, + additional 1 tablespoon, if needed

1 cup whole-wheat flour

1 tablespoon + 1 teaspoon olive oil

2 teaspoons salt

INSTRUCTIONS

Place the yeast and sugar in a small bowl. Add the lukewarm water. Stir gently to mix. Allow to sit for 5 minutes, until it becomes foamy.

In a mixer fitted with a dough hook, add the flours, olive oil, and salt. Add the yeast-water mixture and mix on low until dough comes together. Raise the mixer speed to medium and mix for 3 to 5 minutes. If dough seems too dry, add water 1 tablespoon at a time, taking care not to add too much water.

This dough should be on the more firm side. If it's still sticky, you can add 1 tablespoon flour.

Allow dough to rise in a greased bowl for 2 hours with a towel draped on top.

Preheat oven to 500°F and place the pizza stone on the top rack of oven to heat. Leave pizza stone in heated oven for at least 30 minutes.

Divide the dough into 6 to 8 even pieces (use a food scale to measure most precisely).

Roll each piece into a smooth ball and place on a baking sheet lined with parchment paper or silicone baking mat. Drape a towel over the baking sheet and allow to sit for another 30 minutes.

Roll out each piece of dough into a flat, round disc around 3 inches wide and ½ inch thick, using a rolling pin. Keep remaining balls of dough covered while you are working.

In batches of one or two, place flattened disc on pizza stone at back of oven. Watching closely, bake for 3 minutes or until pita has puffed up. Flip onto other side and bake for another 30 to 60 seconds.

Using metal tongs, remove pita from oven and wrap immediately in a towel. Repeat with remaining dough until all the pitas have baked. Keep pita wrapped in a towel until it has completely cooled. If you place still-warm pita in a plastic bag or container, condensation will form and the bread will get soggy.

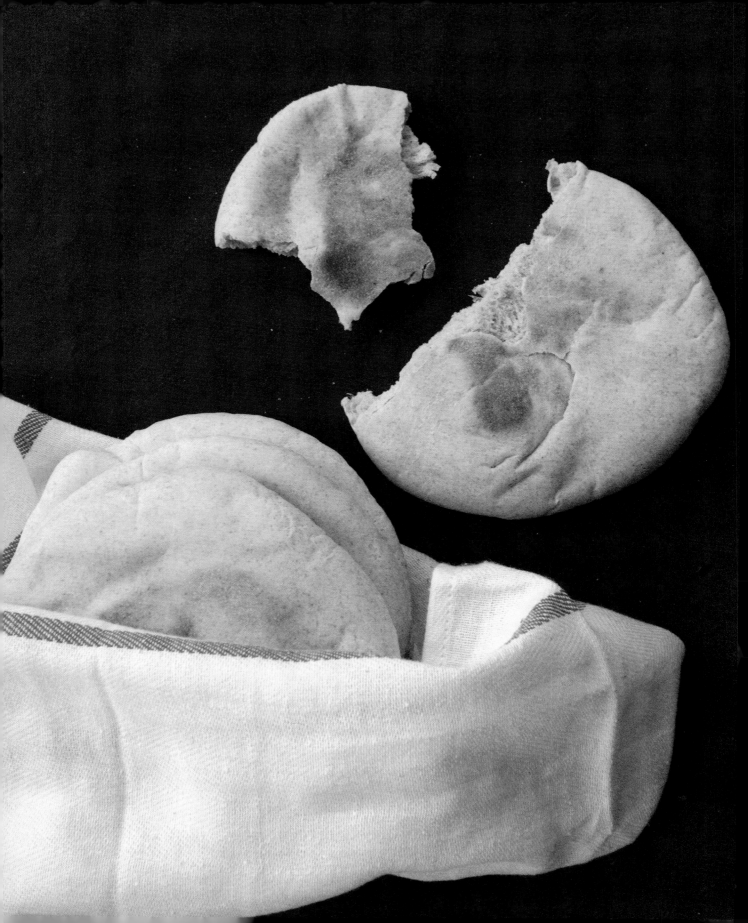

GARLIC PITA

Pita is pretty perfect all on its own. But add a little garlic to the mix and the result is a special pita that is an ideal complement to hummus, soups, or stew.

Yields 6 to 8 pieces

INGREDIENTS

2 teaspoons yeast

½ teaspoon sugar

1 cup + 1 tablespoon lukewarm water

2 cups + 2 teaspoons all-purpose flour

1 cup whole-wheat flour

1 tablespoon + 1 teaspoon olive oil

2 teaspoons salt

2 teaspoons jarred minced garlic in oil

INSTRUCTIONS

Place the yeast and sugar in a small bowl. Add the lukewarm water and stir gently to mix. Allow to sit for 5 minutes, until it becomes foamy.

In a mixer fitted with a dough hook, add the flours, olive oil, salt, and garlic. Add the yeast-water mixture and mix on low until dough comes together. Raise the mixer speed to medium and mix for 3 to 5 minutes. If the dough seems too dry, add water 1 tablespoon at a time, taking care not to add too much water.

This dough should be on the more firm side. If it's still sticky, you can add 1 tablespoon flour. Allow dough to rise in a greased bowl for 2 hours with a towel draped on top.

Preheat oven to 500°F and place the pizza stone on the top rack of oven to heat. Leave pizza stone in heated oven for at least 30 minutes.

Divide the dough into 6 to 8 even pieces (use a food scale to measure most precisely).

Roll each piece into a smooth ball and place on a baking sheet lined with parchment paper or silicone baking mat. Drape a towel over the baking sheet and allow to sit for another 30 minutes.

Roll out each piece of dough into a flat, round disc around 3 inches wide and ½ inch thick, using a rolling pin. Keep remaining balls of dough covered while you are working.

In batches of one or two, place flattened disc on pizza stone at back of oven. Watching closely, bake for 3 minutes or until pita has puffed up. Flip onto other side and bake for another 30 to 60 seconds.

Using metal tongs, remove pita from oven and wrap immediately in a towel. Repeat with remaining dough until all pitas have baked. Keep pita wrapped in towel until it has completely cooled. If you place still-warm pita in a plastic bag or container, condensation will form and the bread will get soggy.

ZA'ATAR PITA

You can find za'atar on top of flatbreads and pita throughout Israel. In this recipe I add za'atar to the dough itself and then add extra on top for flavor and crunch. It's delicious on its own, but is even more delicious when it's dipped right into some hummus or other spreads.

Yields 6 to 8 pieces

INGREDIENTS

2 teaspoons yeast

½ teaspoon sugar

1 cup + 1 tablespoon lukewarm water

2 cups all-purpose flour, + 1 additional tablespoon, if needed

1 cup whole-wheat flour

3 tablespoons + 1 teaspoon olive oil

2 teaspoons salt

2 tablespoons + 2 teaspoons za'atar

INSTRUCTIONS

Place the yeast and sugar in a small bowl. Add the lukewarm water and stir gently to mix. Allow to sit for 5 minutes, until it becomes foamy.

In a mixer fitted with a dough hook, add the flours, 1 tablespoon plus 1 teaspoon of the olive oil, salt, and 2 teaspoons of the za'atar. Add the yeast-water mixture and mix on low until dough comes together. Raise mixer speed to medium and mix for 3 to 5 minutes. If dough seems too dry, add water 1 tablespoon at a time, taking care not to add too much water.

This dough should be on the more firm side. If it's still sticky, you can add 1 tablespoon flour.

Allow dough to rise in a greased bowl for 2 hours with a towel draped on top.

Preheat oven to 500°F and place pizza stone on top rack of oven to heat. Leave pizza stone in heated oven for at least 30 minutes.

Divide the dough into 6 to 8 even pieces (use a food scale to measure most precisely).

Roll each piece into a smooth ball and place on a baking sheet lined with parchment paper or silicone baking mat. Drape a towel over the baking sheet and allow to sit for another 30 minutes.

Mix the remaining 2 tablespoons za'atar and 2 tablespoons olive oil in a small bowl. Roll out each piece of dough into a flat, round disc around 3 inches wide and ½ inch thick, using a rolling pin. After rolling out each piece of pita, brush the za'atar mix on top of pita. Keep the remaining balls of dough covered while you are working.

In batches of one or two, place flattened disc on pizza stone at back of oven. Watching closely, bake for 3 minutes or until pita has puffed up. Flip onto other side and bake for another 30 to 60 seconds.

Using metal tongs, remove pita from oven and wrap immediately in a towel. Repeat with remaining dough until all pitas have baked. Keep the pita wrapped in a towel until it has completely cooled. If you place still-warm pita in a plastic bag or container, condensation will form and the bread will get soggy.

SAFFRON PITA

In this recipe, saffron imparts a subtle spice and a beautiful color without being overwhelming. Saffron is not difficult to find these days—you can find it in most spice aisles at the supermarket or from online retailers.

Yields 6 to 8 pieces

INGREDIENTS

2 teaspoons yeast

½ teaspoon sugar

½ teaspoon saffron threads

1 cup + 1 tablespoon lukewarm water

2 cups all-purpose flour, + 1 additional tablespoon, if needed

1 cup whole-wheat flour

1 tablespoon + 1 teaspoon olive oil

2 teaspoons salt

INSTRUCTIONS

Place the yeast, sugar, and saffron threads in a small bowl. Add the lukewarm water and stir gently to mix. Allow to sit for 5 minutes, until it becomes foamy.

In a mixer fitted with a dough hook, add the flours, olive oil, and salt. Add the yeast-water mixture and mix on low until dough comes together. Raise the mixer speed to medium and mix for 3 to 5 minutes. If the dough seems too dry, add water 1 tablespoon at a time, taking care not to add too much water. This dough should be on the more firm side. If it's still sticky, you can add 1 tablespoon flour.

Allow dough to rise in a greased bowl for 2 hours with a towel draped on top.

Preheat oven to 500°F and place pizza stone on top rack of oven to heat. Leave pizza stone in heated oven for at least 30 minutes.

Divide the dough into 6 to 8 even pieces (use a food scale to measure most precisely). Roll each piece into a smooth ball and place on a baking sheet lined with parchment paper or silicone baking mat. Drape a towel over the baking sheet and allow to sit for another 30 minutes.

Roll out each piece of dough into a flat, round disc around 3 inches wide and ½ inch thick, using a rolling pin. Keep remaining balls of dough covered while you are working.

In batches of one or two, place flattened disc on pizza stone at back of oven. Watching closely, bake for 3 minutes or until pita has puffed up. Flip onto other side and bake for another 30 to 60 seconds.

Using metal tongs, remove pita from oven and wrap immediately in a towel. Repeat with the remaining dough until all pitas have baked. Keep pita wrapped in a towel until it has completely cooled. If you place still-warm pita in a plastic bag or container, condensation will form and the bread will get soggy.

LEFTOVER REMIX: PITA CHIPS

I never want to throw out leftover bread, especially when it's homemade. Cut your day-old pita into triangles, and then toss with olive oil, salt, and pepper to create a truly scratch-made treat for noshing anytime.

Yields about 3 cups of chips

INGREDIENTS

2 leftover pitas

2 tablespoons olive oil

Salt and pepper to taste

INSTRUCTIONS

Preheat oven to 375°F. Cut pita bread into triangles.

Spread in an even layer on a baking sheet. Drizzle with olive oil and salt and pepper. Mix with hands until coated.

Bake for 10 minutes on one side. Flip over and cook another 3 to 6 minutes on the other, to your desired level of crispiness.

HAVE WITH: CLASSIC HUMMUS

America has truly embraced hummus in the past ten years—you can find it in large size containers in every supermarket and in snack-size portions at gas stations. This hummus recipe, which is a shortcut version that does not involve cooking the chickpeas, only takes about 5 minutes to put together. I recommend getting the best quality tahini you can find. I have found that removing the skins off the chickpeas creates a smoother result, but you can skip this step if you prefer chunkier hummus.

Yields 4 to 6 servings

INGREDIENTS

1 (15-ounce) can chickpeas, rinsed and shells removed

¼ cup tahini

½ teaspoon cumin

½ teaspoon salt

2 whole garlic cloves

½ cup olive oil, + additional, for serving

2–3 tablespoons water

Paprika (optional), for garnish

Za'atar (optional), for garnish

INSTRUCTIONS

Place chickpeas, tahini, cumin, salt, and garlic cloves in a food processor fitted with a blade attachment. Pulse for 30 seconds.

Add olive oil and process until smooth. Add water one tablespoon at a time until desired smoothness.

Spoon onto plate or into a bowl. Top with paprika or za'atar and an extra drizzle of olive oil for serving. Can be kept in an airtight container for 5 to 7 days in a refrigerator.

This recipe originally appeared on the blog The Nosher.

HAVE WITH: YOGURT BEET DIP

The bright pink color of this dip is absolutely mesmerizing. If you don't have time to roast the beets, let them cool, and then purée them, don't worry. You can use an alternative: beets in the form of store-bought baby food or canned beets.

Yields 4 to 6 servings

INGREDIENTS

1 large beet, trimmed

½ cup Greek yogurt

1 tablespoon tahini

½ teaspoon salt

¼ teaspoon pepper

¼ teaspoon cumin

INSTRUCTIONS

Preheat oven to 400°F. Wrap the beet in foil and roast for 45 to 60 minutes, or until nearly soft. Allow to cool slightly. Remove skin.

Place the beet in a food processor fitted with a blade and process until completely smooth. Add the yogurt, tahini, and spices.

HAVE WITH: WHITE BEAN AND HERB DIP

This white bean dip is like an Italian version of hummus, and like my hummus recipe it only takes 5 minutes to throw together. You could use either the larger cannellini beans or the small Northern white beans. Add whatever herb mix you like and purée until it is the desired consistency.

Yields 4 to 6 servings

INGREDIENTS

1 (15-ounce) can cannellini beans (or other white bean)

¼ cup fresh chopped parsley, + additional, for serving

2 garlic cloves

½ teaspoon salt

¼ teaspoon pepper

⅓ cup olive oil, + additional, for serving

2–3 tablespoons water

INSTRUCTIONS

Place beans, parsley, garlic, salt, and pepper in a food processor fitted with a blade attachment. Start processing.

Add olive oil and process until smooth. Add water one tablespoon at a time until desired smoothness.

Serve with fresh parsley and additional olive oil on top.

LEFTOVER REMIX: FATTOUSH SALAD WITH SUMAC PITA CHIPS

Fattoush salad is the Middle Eastern version of panzanella, or day-old bread salad. Flavored with sumac, a slightly tart spice with a beautiful maroon hue, pomegranate molasses, lemon juice, and fresh herbs, this fattoush salad is both hearty and refreshing. It's perfect during the summertime when fresh tomatoes and cucumbers are in abundance, and it's a great way to use up pita that is past its prime.

Yields 4 servings

INGREDIENTS

FOR THE PITA CHIPS:

1 leftover pita, cut into triangles

1–2 tablespoons olive oil

½ teaspoon sumac

Salt and pepper to taste

FOR THE SALAD:

2 bunches romaine lettuce, chopped

3 roma tomatoes, diced, or 2 cups cherry tomatoes, halved

1 English cucumber, cut into medium chunks

¼ red onion, chopped

¼ cup fresh chopped parsley

¼ cup fresh chopped mint

FOR THE DRESSING:

Juice of ½ lemon

½ teaspoon sumac

2 teaspoons pomegranate molasses

Salt and pepper to taste

½ cup olive oil

INSTRUCTIONS

Preheat oven to 375°F.

Spread pita triangles on an ungreased baking sheet. Drizzle with 1 to 2 tablespoons olive oil, ½ teaspoon sumac, and salt and pepper. Mix with hands until pita is coated.

Bake for 10 minutes on one side. Flip over and bake for another 5 to 7 minutes on the other. Remove from oven and allow to cool.

To assemble salad, place lettuce, tomatoes, cucumber, red onion, parsley, and mint in a large bowl.

In a smaller bowl, whisk together lemon juice, ½ teaspoon sumac, pomegranate molasses, salt, pepper, and olive oil until emulsified.

Break up pita chips with hands roughly and place on salad. Pour salad dressing on top and toss until coated. Serve immediately.

MATZAH

The story of matzah is no great secret: The Jews had to leave Egypt in a hurry and didn't have time for their dough to rise. And so matzah, and the holiday of Passover, was born. Matzah is a flat, typically bland cracker made simply of flour, water, oil, and salt. For some Jews it is beloved, and evokes a deep sense of family, tradition, and pride. For others, it is an annual, ritualistic necessity. And for others, like my non-Jewish mother, it is a staple. She just loved to eat matzah for breakfast year-round with butter.

Homemade matzah is very different than the boxed variety. It takes well to different seasonings, and is far more flavorful than the store-bought variety. It's also incredibly simple: no rising and almost no fancy equipment is necessary. If you don't have a pasta machine or a pasta attachment, simply roll out the dough as thin as you can get it using a heavy rolling pin.

HOW THE DOUGH SHOULD FEEL

The dough should be on the firmer side, not too elastic, and should not feel sticky.

ESSENTIAL TOOLS

Rolling pin for rolling the dough

Pasta machine or attachment

Fork

Pizza stone for baking

SPECIAL NOTES

If you plan to make matzah for Passover, according to tradition it should only take 18 minutes from the start of making the dough to baking. For this reason, a smaller batch of dough is used in these recipes. But you can easily double or triple these recipes to make bigger batches of matzah.

SHAPING MATZAH

BASIC MATZAH

This homemade matzah is nothing like the boxed variety. Homemade matzah will more closely resemble a flatbread or cracker than traditional matzah, and you can easily add a variety of flavors. It will dazzle your guests for Passover, and can serve as the perfect accompaniment to a cheese platter year-round.

Yields 8 to 10 large matzah crackers

INGREDIENTS

1 cup flour, + additional
1–2 tablespoons, if needed

¼ teaspoon salt

½ tablespoon olive oil

¼ cup + 1 tablespoon warm water

INSTRUCTIONS

Preheat oven to 500°F. Place pizza stone in the oven to heat on top rack.

Combine flour, salt, olive oil, and water in a medium bowl. Mix until smooth dough forms. If the dough feels too sticky after mixing, add another 1 to 2 tablespoons of flour.

Cut dough into four parts and roll out each piece with a rolling pin.

Flatten each piece and pass it repeatedly through a pasta maker or attachment, starting at level 8 or 9 and going until level 4 or 5. If you do not have a pasta maker, roll out dough using a rolling pin until you get it as thin as possible.

Using a pizza cutter or dough cutter, cut each dough in half to form squares. Poke holes in even lines all over the dough using a fork.

Place squares into oven on top of pizza stone in batches. Bake on first side for 2 to 3 minutes. Turn over and cook 1 more minute, or until edges are starting to brown but not burn.

Allow to cool. Can be stored in airtight container for 1 to 2 weeks.

SWEET CINNAMON MATZAH

A slightly sweet matzah is the perfect vehicle for a Passover breakfast of cream cheese or butter. Or top with chocolate spread and some sliced bananas for snack time.

Yields 8 to 10 large matzah crackers

INGREDIENTS

1 cup flour, + additional
1–2 tablespoons, if needed

¼ teaspoon salt

½ tablespoon olive oil

¼ cup + 1 tablespoon warm water

½ teaspoon vanilla

¼ teaspoon cinnamon

½ teaspoon sugar

INSTRUCTIONS

Preheat oven to 500°F. Place pizza stone in the oven to heat on top rack.

Combine flour, salt, olive oil, water, vanilla, cinnamon, and sugar in a medium bowl. Mix until smooth dough forms. If the dough feels too sticky after mixing, add another 1 to 2 tablespoons of flour.

Cut dough into four parts and roll out each piece with a rolling pin.

Flatten each piece and pass it repeatedly through a pasta maker or attachment, starting at a level 8 or 9 and going until level 4 or 5. If you do not have a pasta maker, roll out dough using a rolling pin until you get it as thin as possible.

Using a pizza cutter or dough cutter, cut dough in half to form squares. Poke holes in even lines all over the dough using a fork.

Place squares into oven on top of pizza stone in batches. Bake on first side for 2 to 3 minutes. Turn over and cook 1 more minute, or until edges are starting to brown but not burn.

Allow to cool. Can be stored in airtight container for 1 to 2 weeks.

TURMERIC MATZAH

I love the smell and color of turmeric, which is also a super healthful spice. This colorful matzah will be a bright and unexpected treat on your Passover table.

Yields 8 to 10 large matzah crackers

INGREDIENTS

1 cup flour, + additional
1–2 tablespoons, if needed

¼ teaspoon salt

½ tablespoon olive oil

¼ cup + 1 tablespoon warm water

½ teaspoon turmeric

INSTRUCTIONS

Preheat oven to 500°F. Place pizza stone in the oven to heat on top rack.

Combine flour, salt, olive oil, water, and turmeric in a medium bowl. Mix until smooth dough forms. If the dough feels too sticky after mixing, add another 1 to 2 tablespoons of flour.

Cut dough into four parts and roll out each piece with a rolling pin.

Flatten each piece and pass it repeatedly through a pasta maker or attachment, starting at a level 8 or 9 and going until level 4 or 5. If you do not have a pasta maker, roll out dough using a rolling pin until you get it as thin as possible.

Using a pizza cutter or dough cutter, cut dough in half to form squares. Poke holes in even lines all over the dough using a fork.

Place squares into oven on top of pizza stone in batches. Bake on first side for 2 to 3 minutes. Turn over and cook 1 more minute, or until edges are starting to brown but not burn.

Allow to cool. Can be stored in airtight container for 1 to 2 weeks.

GARLIC AND HERB MATZAH

The flavor of this matzah is subtle and is unlike any traditional matzah you've tasted. You'll want to eat this with cheese or other spreads all year. It's that good.

Yields 8 to 10 large matzah crackers

INGREDIENTS

1 cup flour, + additional 1–2 tablespoons, if needed

¼ teaspoon salt

½ tablespoon olive oil

¼ cup + 1 tablespoon warm water

¼ teaspoon dried oregano

¼ teaspoon dried basil

1 teaspoon jarred chopped garlic

INSTRUCTIONS

Preheat oven to 500°F. Place pizza stone in the oven to heat on top rack.

Combine flour, salt, olive oil, water, oregano, basil, and garlic in a medium bowl. Mix until smooth dough forms. If the dough feels too sticky after mixing, add another 1 to 2 tablespoons of flour.

Cut dough into four parts and roll out each piece with a rolling pin.

Flatten each piece and pass it repeatedly through a pasta maker or attachment, starting at a level 8 or 9 and going until level 4 or 5. If you do not have a pasta maker, roll out dough using a rolling pin until you get it as thin as possible.

Using a pizza cutter or dough cutter, cut dough in half to form squares. Poke holes in even lines all over the dough using a fork.

Place squares into oven on top of pizza stone in batches. Bake on first side for 2 to 3 minutes. Turn over and cook 1 more minute, or until edges are starting to brown but not burn.

Allow to cool. Can be stored in airtight container for 1 to 2 weeks.

ZA'ATAR MATZAH

Like za'atar pita, this matzah recipe adds za'atar spice into the dough and sprinkles it again on top. I love the color, the crunch, and the flavor of this matzah.

Yields 8 to 10 large matzah crackers

INGREDIENTS

1 cup flour, + additional 1–2 tablespoons, if needed

¼ teaspoon salt

½ tablespoon olive oil, + additional, for topping

¼ cup + 1 tablespoon warm water

½ teaspoon za'atar, + additional, for topping

INSTRUCTIONS

Preheat oven to 500°F. Place pizza stone in the oven to warm on top rack.

Combine flour, salt, olive oil, water, and za'atar. Mix until smooth dough forms. If the dough feels too sticky after mixing, add another 1 to 2 tablespoons of flour.

Cut dough into four parts and roll out each piece with a rolling pin.

Flatten each piece and pass it repeatedly through a pasta maker or attachment, starting at a level 8 or 9 and going until level 4 or 5. If you do not have a pasta maker, roll out dough using a rolling pin until you get it as thin as possible.

Using a pizza cutter or dough cutter, cut dough in half to form squares. Poke holes in even lines all over the dough using a fork. Brush tops of matzah with a thin layer of olive oil and top with an additional sprinkle of za'atar.

Place squares into oven on top of pizza stone in batches. Bake on first side for 2 to 3 minutes. Turn over and cook 1 more minute, or until edges are starting to brown but not burn.

Allow to cool. Can be stored in airtight container for 1 to 2 weeks.

TRUFFLE MATZAH

This is the fanciest matzah of them all! Create a Passover-friendly cheese board with a selection of cheese, jams, fruits, and homemade matzah crackers for a truly unique spread.

Yields 8 to 10 large matzah crackers

INGREDIENTS

1 cup flour, + additional
1–2 tablespoons, if needed

¼ teaspoon salt

½ tablespoon olive oil

¼ cup + 1 tablespoon warm water

¼–⅓ cup truffle oil, for topping

½ teaspoon coarse sea salt or truffle salt, for topping

INSTRUCTIONS

Preheat oven to 500°F. Place pizza stone in the oven to warm on top rack.

Combine flour, salt, olive oil, and water. Mix until smooth dough forms. If the dough feels too sticky after mixing, add another 1 to 2 tablespoons of flour.

Cut dough into four parts and roll each piece out with rolling pin.

Flatten each piece and pass it repeatedly through a pasta maker or attachment, starting at a level 8 or 9 and going until level 4 or 5. If you do not have a pasta maker, roll out dough using a rolling pin until you get it as thin as possible.

Using a pizza cutter or dough cutter, cut dough in half to form squares. Poke holes in even lines all over the dough using a fork. Brush tops of matzah with a thin layer of truffle oil and top with coarse sea salt.

Place squares into oven on top of pizza stone in batches. Bake on first side for 2 to 3 minutes. Turn over and cook 1 more minute, or until edges are starting to brown but not burn.

Allow to cool. Can be stored in airtight container for 1 to 2 weeks.

HAVE WITH: CHOPPED LIVER

There was always chopped liver served on the Jewish holidays at my grandmother's house, but I was always too skeptical to try it as a kid. On my honeymoon we traveled to Florence, Italy, where I tasted a Tuscan-style chicken liver spread for the first time. I have been hooked on chopped liver ever since. This recipe is sort of a hybrid between the Italian style, which is sweeter and smoother, and the more traditional Jewish-American chopped liver, which is chunkier with hard-boiled eggs and lots of fried onions.

Yields 8 to 10 servings

INGREDIENTS

2 tablespoons olive oil

¼ cup + 1 tablespoon schmaltz (or substitute with same amount of olive oil, if you do not have schmaltz)

1 large onion, or 2 small onions, sliced into rounds

1 pound raw chicken livers

1 tablespoon chopped fresh thyme

½ cup very sweet wine or brandy

2 hard-boiled eggs

Salt and pepper to taste

INSTRUCTIONS

In a large sauté pan over medium-low heat, add the olive oil and 1 tablespoon of the schmaltz. Add onions and sauté for 20 to 25 minutes until onions are completely soft and slightly brown.

Set oven on broil. Spread the livers on a lightly greased baking sheet in an even layer. Broil on first side 3 to 4 minutes. Remove from oven and turn over livers. Broil for another 1 to 2 minutes, until livers are still slightly pink in the inside. Allow to cool.

Place broiled livers, half the onions, the remaining ¼ cup schmaltz, fresh thyme leaves, and wine in a food processor fitted with a blade attachment. Pulse until desired smoothness.

Using an egg slicer, cut the hard-boiled eggs into small pieces. Add remaining onions and hard-boiled eggs into liver mixture. Adjust seasoning to taste.

Note: Schmaltz is the yiddish word for fat, most commonly chicken fat, but it also can be duck fat or goose fat. You can make your own schmaltz by chopping up pieces of chicken skin and sautéing them very low and slow in a large sauté pan with sliced onions and a small amount of water (about 1 teaspoon). When the liquid is a golden color and the chicken skin is browned and crispy, the schmaltz is ready. Remove the skin and onions, which is called gribenes (and is delicious to eat). Pour the schmaltz through a fine mesh sieve into a container for storing, or use right away. Schmaltz can be used to make matzah balls, roast potatoes, kugel, and of course, chopped liver spread. My grandmother swears that rubbing chicken fat on your chest is the ultimate cold remedy, but full disclosure: I have thus far only used it for cooking.

ACKNOWLEDGMENTS

To my dear Smithie Sister Jacqueline, thank you for making this happen. To Danielle F., thank you for the never-ending inspiration. And to my "cousin" Danielle Sarna Praport, you have been the most wonderful colleague and friend for the past ten years. I know we are family and bashert.

To my sister-in-law and collaborator Becca—your talent and vision made this more stunning than I could have ever conceived. Thank you for keeping me in line.

Sage and Jacqui—thank you for making this book so crazy beautiful.

When my former editor Ilana Sichel told me to "just take better pictures" nearly five years ago, I never imagined I would take photos for my own cookbook. Thank you.

Emily Pearl Goodstein, you are truly one of a kind and I am so lucky to call you a friend, colleague, and my official headshot taker.

To EMB, whose impact on my life I could never have realized—thank you for your leadership. I know we'll share a plate of lox together again one day.

To my dad—you ensured I could handle anything thrown my way in this life. To Bubbe Phoebe and Grandpa Eddie, thank you for loving your half-Jewish grandchildren no matter what.

There are not enough thank-yous in this world for my Aunt Kathy and Uncle Barry. Without your love, I don't know where I would be. To Jojo and Poppy, thank you for being my cheerleaders, taste testers, and impromptu babysitters.

To my siblings, Jon and Riana, I love you more than words. This all started with you. To my daughters, I hope you will be proud of your crazy mom one day.

As the editor of a website with writers from all over the world, I have had the privilege to work with dozens and dozens of people who are passionate about food. But Jeffrey Yoskowiz and Liz Alpern are the menschiest of the menschy. Thank you for inspiring me, supporting me, and showing the whole of the Jewish food community the classiest way to play this game.

Thank you to Ann Treistman for giving me a chance, and even letting me bring a baby to meetings. Thank you to Aurora Bell and Devorah Backman for your hard work and limitless patience. Thank you to my agent, Jennifer Cohen, for believing in me.

I truly believe that without good mentors, we cannot reach our potential. And without Ms. McLeod, I know I would never have started on this journey. Thank you for seeing me.

To my mom and to Dana, the strongest women I have known: thank you for pushing me forward, especially when it was hard.

They say behind every great man is a great woman. But in this case, behind every crazy woman is an endlessly patient, loving, and supportive partner. Jonathan—I love you and thank you for everything you do, but especially for the late-night supermarket runs to buy ingredients I forgot. This book literally could not have happened without you.

INDEX

A

almonds, in Peach Almond and White Chocolate Rugelach, 172–73
anchovy fillets, in Mixed Olive Tapenade, 22–23
appetizers
  Onion Jam Babka, 116–17
  See also dips and spreads
apples, in Balsamic Apple Date Stuffed Challah, 68–69
artichokes, in Spinach Artichoke Dip, 86

B

babka, 88–139
  about, 89–90
  Babka French Toast, 139
  Basic Savory Babka, 99–101
  Basic Sweet Babka, 96–98
  Birthday Cake Babka, 129–31
  Buffalo Blue Cheese Babka, 120–22
  Chocolate Babka, 102–4
  Cinnamon Babka, 105–7
  Double Chocolate Cookie Babka, 132–34
  Double Layer Caramel and Chocolate Babka, 135–37
  Fig Jam and Goat Cheese Babka, 127–28
  Guava and Cheese Babka, 118–19
  Olive Tapenade Babka, 124–26
  Onion Jam Babka, 116–17
  Peanut Butter and Jelly Babka, 114–15
  Savory Babka Croutons, 123
  shaping, 92–95

  S'mores Babka, 108–10
  Tropical Babka, 111–13
bagels, 140–61
  about, 141–42
  Basic Bagels, 146–47
  Blueberry Bagels, 156–57
  Cinnamon Raisin Bagels, 158–59
  Gravlax, 155
  Jalapeño Cheddar Bagels, 152–53
  Pizza Bagels, 160–61
  Rye Bagels, 150–51
  shaping, 144–45
  Whole-Wheat Bagels, 148–49
baking techniques, 9
Balsamic Apple Date Stuffed Challah, 68–69
Banana Bread Chocolate Chip Challah, 64–66
Basic Challah Braid, 32–33
basic recipes
  Bagels, 146–47
  Challah, 46–47
  Matzah, 236–37
  Pita Bread, 216–17
  Savory Babka, 99–101
  Savory Hamantaschen, 194–95
  Sweet Babka, 96–98
  Sweet Hamantaschen, 193
  Sweet Rugelach, 166–69
basil
  Kale Basil Walnut Pesto, 20–21
  Tomato Basil Challah, 58–59
beans and legumes. *See* cannellini beans; chickpeas; white beans

beef, in Sloppy Joe Filling, 82–83

Beet Dip, Yogurt, 226–27

Birthday Cake Babka, 129–31

Blueberry Bagels, 156–57

Blue Cheese Babka, Buffalo, 120–22

Bread Pudding, White Chocolate Challah, 75

breads. *See* bagels; challah; pita bread

Brie and Herb Hamantaschen, 208

Buffalo Blue Cheese Babka, 120–22

C

cake. *See* babka

cannellini beans, in White Bean and Herb Dip, 228–29

Caramel and Chocolate Babka, Double Layer, 135–37

caraway seeds, in Rye Bagels, 150–51

challah, 28–87
  about, 29–30
  Balsamic Apple Date Stuffed Challah, 68–69
  Banana Bread Chocolate Chip Challah, 64–66
  Basic Challah, 46–47
  Basic Challah Braid, 32–33
  braiding and shaping, 32–44
  Challah Dogs and Pretzel Challah Dogs, 76–79
  Challah Knots, 40–41
  Chocolate Cherry Challah, 67
  Cinnamon Raisin Challah, 60–61
  8-Strand Round Challah, 38–39
  Everything Bagel Challah, 50–51
  Horseradish and Dill Challah, 56–57
  Onion Challah Rolls, 80–81
  Pesto and Goat Cheese Stuffed Challah, 72–74
  Pull-Apart Challah with Spinach Artichoke Dip, 84–87
  Pumpkin Spice Challah, 70–71

Rosemary Garlic Challah, 52–53

6-Strand Challah Braid, 36–37

Sloppy Joe Filling, 82–83

Stuffed 3-Strand Challah, 42–43

Stuffed Turban Challah, 44–45

3-Strand Round Challah, 34–35

Tomato Basil Challah, 58–59

Walnut Cranberry Raisin Challah, 62–63

White Chocolate Challah Bread Pudding, 75

Whole-Grain Challah, 48–49

Za'atar and Garlic Challah, 54–55

cheddar cheese
  Jalapeño Cheddar Bagels, 152–53
  in Spinach Artichoke Dip, 86

cheese
  Guava and Cheese Babka, 118–19
  See also blue cheese; Brie cheese; cream cheese; goat cheese; mozzarella cheese; Parmesan cheese

Cheesecake Hamantaschen, Coconut, 206–7

cherries, dried, in Chocolate Cherry Challah, 67

chicken livers, in Chopped Liver, 246–47

chickpeas, in Classic Hummus, 224–25

chile peppers, in Jalapeño Cheddar Bagels, 152–53

chocolate
  Banana Bread Chocolate Chip Challah, 64–66
  Chocolate Babka, 102–4
  Chocolate Cherry Challah, 67
  Chocolate Chip Cookie Hamantaschen, 202–3
  Chocolate Dipped Sprinkles Hamantaschen, 196–97
  Chocolate Filling, 26–27
  Chocolate Peppermint Rugelach, 176–78
  Double Chocolate Cookie Babka, 132–34
  Double Layer Caramel and Chocolate Babka, 135–37

Pumpkin Chocolate Hazelnut Rugelach,
170–71
Raspberry Chocolate Rugelach, 174–75
in S'mores Babka filling, 108–10
Triple Chocolate Hamantaschen, 204–5
See also white chocolate
chocolate hazelnut spread
Chocolate Chip Cookie Hamantaschen, 203
S'mores Babka, 108–10
Triple Chocolate Hamantaschen, 204–5
Chopped Liver, 246–47
cinnamon
Cinnamon Babka, 105–7
Cinnamon Raisin Bagels, 158–59
Cinnamon Raisin Challah, 60–61
Cinnamon Sugar Filling, 24–25
in Pumpkin Spice Challah, 70–71
in Spiced Sugar, 16–17
Sweet Cinnamon Matzah, 238–39
Classic Hummus, 224–25
coconut
Coconut Cheesecake Hamantaschen,
206–7
in Tropical Babka, 111–13
condiments
harissa, in rugelach, 185
Kale Basil Walnut Pesto, 20–21
Mixed Olive Tapenade, 22–23
Savory Onion Jam, 22–23
cookies, Oreo, in Double Chocolate Cookie
Babka, 132–34
cookies, types of. *See* hamantaschen;
rugelach
crackers. *See* graham crackers; matzah
cranberries, in Walnut Cranberry Raisin
Challah, 62–63
cream cheese
Basic Savory Rugelach, 168–69
Basic Sweet Rugelach, 166–67
Chocolate Peppermint Rugelach, 176–78
Coconut Cheesecake Hamantaschen,
206–7

Everything Bagel Rugelach, 182–83
filling, in Birthday Cake Babka, 129–31
filling, in Coconut Cheesecake
Hamantaschen, 206–7
filling, in Double Chocolate Cookie Babka,
134
filling, in Guava and Cheese Babka, 118–19
Harissa and Goat Cheese Rugelach,
184–85
Peach Almond and White Chocolate
Rugelach, 172–73
Pesto Parmesan Rugelach, 179
Pumpkin Chocolate Hazelnut Rugelach,
170–71
Raspberry Chocolate Rugelach, 174–75
Spicy Pizza Rugelach, 180–81
Tropical Babka filling, 111–13
Croutons, Savory Babka, 123
crumb topping
basic recipe, 18–19
for Birthday Cake Babka, 131
cucumber, in Fattoush Salad with Sumac
Pita Chips, 230–31
cumin, in dips, 225, 227

D

dates, in Balsamic Apple Date Stuffed
Challah, 68–69
desserts. *See* babka; Bread Pudding;
rugelach
dill
in Everything Bagel Rugelach, 182–83
in Gravlax, 155
Horseradish and Dill Challah, 56–57
dips and spreads
Chopped Liver, 246–47
Classic Hummus, 224–25
Spinach Artichoke Dip with Pull-Apart
Challah, 84–87
White Bean and Herb Dip, 228–29
Yogurt Beet Dip, 226–27

Double Chocolate Cookie Babka, 132–34
dough, braiding and shaping
    babka, 92–95
    bagels, 144–45
    challah, 32–43
    hamantaschen, 190–91
    matzah, 234–35
    pita, 214–15
    rugelach, 164–65
dough, rising of, 9
dressings
    pomegranate sumac, 230
dulce de leche, in hamantaschen filling, 203

E

eggs, in Chopped Liver, 246–47
8-Strand Round Challah, 38–39
equipment. *See* tools for baking
Everything Bagel Challah, 50–51
Everything Bagel Rugelach, 182–83
Everything Bagel Topping, 14–15

F

Fattoush Salad with Sumac Pita Chips,
    230–31
Fig Jam and Goat Cheese Babka, 127–28
filling(s)
    apple and date, 68
    blue cheese, 121
    caramel, 137
    chocolate, 26–27
    chocolate hazelnut as, 203
    cinnamon sugar, 24–25, 105
    cookie butter as, 203
    cream cheese, 111, 129, 182, 206
    cream cheese and guava, 118
    cream cheese and Oreo, 134
    dulce de leche as, 203
    fig jam and goat cheese, 127
    kale and pesto, 99

Kale Basil Walnut Pesto, 20–21
Mixed Olive Tapenade as, 125
peanut butter and jelly, 114
pesto and goat cheese, 74
Savory Onion Jam as, 116
Sloppy Joe, 83
s'mores, 109
fish. *See* anchovy fillets; salmon
flaxseed, in toppings, 49, 63
flour, 9
    See also rye; whole-wheat flour
French Toast, Babka, 138–39
frostings
    confectioners' sugar, 131

G

garlic
    in Everything Bagel Topping, 14–15
    Garlic and Herb Matzah, 242–43
    Garlic Pita, 218–19
    Rosemary Garlic Challah, 52–53
    Za'atar and Garlic Challah, 54–55
goat cheese
    Fig Jam and Goat Cheese Babka, 127–28
    Harissa and Goat Cheese Rugelach, 184–85
    Onion Jam and Goat Cheese
        Hamantaschen, 209
    Pesto and Goat Cheese Stuffed Challah,
        72–74
    in Spinach Artichoke Dip, 86
graham crackers, in s'mores recipes, 108–10,
    199–201
Grape Jelly, Rye Crust Hamantaschen with,
    210–11
Gravlax, 155
Guava and Cheese Babka, 118–19

H

hamantaschen, 186–211
    about, 187–88

Basic Savory Hamantaschen, 194–95
Basic Sweet Hamantaschen, 192–93
Brie and Herb Hamantaschen, 208
Chocolate Chip Cookie Hamantaschen, 202–3
Chocolate Dipped Sprinkles Hamantaschen, 196–97
Coconut Cheesecake Hamantaschen, 206–7
Onion Jam and Goat Cheese Hamantaschen, 209
Rye Crust Hamantaschen with Grape Jelly, 210–11
shaping, 190–91
S'mores Hamantaschen, 199–201
Triple Chocolate Hamantaschen, 204–5
Harissa and Goat Cheese Rugelach, 184–85
Hazelnut Rugelach, Pumpkin Chocolate, 170–71
hazelnut spread. *See* chocolate hazelnut spread
herbes de Provence
    Brie and Herb Hamantaschen, 208
    in Fig Jam and Goat Cheese Babka, 127–28
Herb Matzah, Garlic and, 242–43
    See also specific herbs
horseradish
    in Gravlax, 155
    Horseradish and Dill Challah, 56–57
Hummus, Classic, 224–25
    See also White Bean and Herb Dip

J

Jalapeño Cheddar Bagels, 152–53
jam
    filling, in Hamantaschen, 193, 197
    Savory Onion Jam, 22–23
jellies

Grape Jelly, Rye Crust Hamantaschen with, 210–11
Peanut Butter and Jelly Babka, 114–15

K

kale
    in babka filling, 99
    Kale Basil Walnut Pesto, 20–21

L

leftover remixes
    Babka French Toast, 139
    Fattoush Salad with Sumac Pita Chips, 230–31
    Pita Chips, 223
    Pizza Bagels, 160–61
    Savory Babka Croutons, 123
    White Chocolate Challah Bread Pudding, 75

M

malt barley, 142
marshmallow, in s'mores fillings, 109–10, 199–200
matzah, 232–47
    about, 233
    Basic Matzah, 236–37
    Chopped Liver, 246–47
    Garlic and Herb Matzah, 242–43
    shaping, 234–35
    Sweet Cinnamon Matzah, 238–39
    Truffle Matzah, 244–45
    Turmeric Matzah, 240–41
    Za'atar Matzah, 243
mint, in Fattoush Salad with Sumac Pita Chips, 230–31
Mixed Olive Tapenade, 22–23
mozzarella cheese
    in babka topping, 99
    Spicy Pizza Rugelach, 180–81

N

nuts and seeds. *See* almonds; peanut
butter; seeds; walnuts

O

olives
Mixed Olive Tapenade, 22–23
Olive Tapenade Babka, 124–26
onions
Onion Challah Rolls, 80–81
Onion Jam and Goat Cheese
Hamantaschen, 209
Onion Jam Babka, 116–17
Savory Onion Jam, 22–23
oven temperatures, 9

P

Parmesan cheese
Pesto Parmesan Rugelach, 179
Spinach Artichoke Dip, 86
pastries. *See* babka; hamantaschen;
rugelach
Peach Almond and White Chocolate
Rugelach, 172–73
Peanut Butter and Jelly Babka, 114–15
pepitas (pumpkin seeds), in toppings, 71
peppermint bark, in Chocolate Peppermint
Rugelach, 176–78
pesto
Kale Basil Walnut Pesto, 20–21
Pesto and Goat Cheese Stuffed Challah,
72–74
Pesto Parmesan Rugelach, 179
pineapple, in Tropical Babka, 111–13
pita bread, 212–31
about, 213
Basic Pita Bread, 216–17
Classic Hummus, 224–25

Fattoush Salad with Sumac Pita Chips,
230–31
Garlic Pita, 218–19
Pita Chips, 223
Saffron Pita, 222
shaping, 214–15
White Bean and Herb Dip, 228–29
Yogurt Beet Dip, 226–27
Za'atar Pita, 220–21
pita chips
basic recipe, 223
Sumac Pita Chips, Fattoush Salad with,
230–31
Pizza Bagels, 160–61
Pizza Rugelach, Spicy, 180–81
pomegranate sumac dressing, 230–31
poppy seeds, in toppings, 14, 47
Pretzel Challah Dogs, 78
Pull-Apart Challah with Spinach Artichoke
Dip, 84–87
Pumpkin Chocolate Hazelnut Rugelach,
170–71
Pumpkin Spice Challah, 70–71

R

raisins
Cinnamon Raisin Bagels, 158–59
Cinnamon Raisin Challah, 60–61
Walnut Cranberry Raisin Challah, 62–63
Raspberry Chocolate Rugelach, 174–75
Rolls, Onion Challah, 80–81
Rosemary Garlic Challah, 52–53
rugelach, 162–85
about, 163
Basic Savory Rugelach, 168–69
Basic Sweet Rugelach, 166–67
Chocolate Peppermint Rugelach, 176–78
Everything Bagel Rugelach, 182–83
Harissa and Goat Cheese Rugelach,
184–85

Peach Almond and White Chocolate Rugelach, 172–73

Pesto Parmesan Rugelach, 179

Pumpkin Chocolate Hazelnut Rugelach, 170–71

Raspberry Chocolate Rugelach, 174–75

shaping, 164–65

Spicy Pizza Rugelach, 180–81

Rye Bagels, 150–51

Rye Crust Hamantaschen with Grape Jelly, 210–11

S

Saffron Pita, 222

salad dressings

pomegranate sumac, 230

salads

Fattoush Salad with Sumac Pita Chips, 230–31

salmon, in Gravlax, 155

Savory Babka, Basic, 99–101

Savory Babka Croutons, 123

Savory Hamantaschen, Basic, 194–95

Savory Rugelach, Basic, 168–69

Savory Onion Jam, 22–23

seeds

in bagel topping, 14

types of, 13

See also specific seeds

sesame seeds, in toppings, 14, 47, 86

6-Strand Challah Braid, 36–37

Sloppy Joe Filling, 82–83

S'mores Babka, 108–10

S'mores Hamantaschen, 199–201

spice blends. *See* za'atar

Spiced Sugar, 16–17

Spicy Pizza Rugelach, 180–81

Spinach Artichoke Dip, Pull-Apart Challah with, 84–87

spreads. *See* dips and spreads

Sprinkles Hamantaschen, Chocolate Dipped, 196–97

Stuffed 3-Strand Challah, 42–43

Stuffed Turban Challah, 44–45

sugar

Cinnamon Sugar Filling, 24–25

Spiced Sugar, 16–17

sumac

in salad dressing, 230

Sumac Pita Chips, Fattoush Salad with, 230–31

in Za'atar and Garlic Challah, 54–55

sunflower seeds, in toppings, 49, 63

Sweet Babka, Basic, 96–98

Sweet Cinnamon Matzah, 238–39

Sweet Hamantaschen, Basic, 193

Sweet Rugelach, Basic, 166–69

T

tahini

Classic Hummus, 224–25

Yogurt Beet Dip, 226–27

tapenade

Mixed Olive Tapenade, 22–23

Olive Tapenade Babka, 124–26

techniques. *See* baking techniques; dough, braiding and shaping

3-Strand Round Challah, 34–35

thyme, in Chopped Liver, 246–47

tomatoes

Fattoush Salad with Sumac Pita Chips, 230–31

Spicy Pizza Rugelach, 180–81

Tomato Basil Challah, 58–59

tools for baking, 9–11

toppings

Crumb Topping, 18–19, 131

Everything Bagel Topping, 14–15

Spiced Sugar, 16–17

types of, 13

Triple Chocolate Hamantaschen, 204–5
Tropical Babka, 111–13
Truffle Matzah, 244–45
Turmeric Matzah, 240–41

W

walnuts
  Kale Basil Walnut Pesto, 20–21
  Walnut Cranberry Raisin Challah, 62–63
White Bean and Herb Dip, 228–29
white chocolate
  Chocolate Peppermint Rugelach, 176–78
  Peach Almond and White Chocolate
    Rugelach, 172–73
  in Tropical Babka topping, 111–12
  White Chocolate Challah Bread Pudding,
    75
Whole-Grain Challah, 48–49
whole-wheat flour

Basic Pita Bread, 216–17
Garlic Pita, 218–19
Saffron Pita, 222
Walnut Cranberry Raisin Challah, 62–63
Whole-Grain Challah, 48–49
Whole-Wheat Bagels, 148–49
Za'atar Pita, 220–21
wine, sweet, in Chopped Liver, 246–47

Y

Yogurt Beet Dip, 226–27

Z

za'atar
  about, 55
  and Garlic Challah, 54–55
  Za'atar Matzah, 243
  Za'atar Pita, 220–21

ABOUT THE AUTHOR

Born to an Italian mother who loved to bake, a Jewish father who loved to experiment, and a food-chemist grandfather, loving and experimenting with diverse foods is simply in Shannon Sarna's blood. And so is music and performance: her mother, father, uncle, and brother are all musicians. Sarna studied classical piano, dance, and voice, and performed in local and regional musical theatre until age 17. She went on to study Spanish, French, Russian, and comparative government at Smith College in Northampton, MA. After college she lived in Washington, DC, worked briefly for a political lobbying firm, but soon after began working in the non-profit field. Sarna moved back to New York in 2007 to work for renowned philanthropist, Edgar M. Bronfman, of blessed memory, during which time her passion for writing, social media, and food was truly awakened. She went on to launch *The Nosher* with MyJewishLearning, now part of 70 Faces Media, where she manages daily content, corresponds with contributors from around the world, produces weekly food videos featuring Jewish and Israeli–inspired recipes, news, and round-ups. Sarna has written for *Tablet Magazine*, *Vinepair*, *Modern Loss*, *New Jersey Monthly Magazine*, and *Joy of Kosher Magazine*. She dreams of owning her own farm one day and, in the meantime, enjoys spinning, gardening, drinking with her mom friends, and chasing after her cute but ill-behaved children and rescue dogs in South Orange, NJ.

371 2975

For information about permission to reproduce selections from this book, write to
Permissions, The Countryman Press, 500 Fifth Avenue, New York, NY 10110

For information about special discounts for bulk purchases, please contact
W. W. Norton Special Sales at specialsales@wwnorton.com or 800-233-4830

Manufacturing by LSC Communications, Willard
Book design by Becca Goldberg, Suite Paperie
Junior designer: Jacqui McCullough
Production manager: Devon Zahn

The Countryman Press
www.countrymanpress.com

A division of W. W. Norton & Company, Inc.
500 Fifth Avenue, New York, NY 10110
www.wwnorton.com

978-1-68268-021-6

10 9 8 7 6 5 4 3 2 1